The Backyard Peace Project
Volume One

Compiled by Cathy Domoney

Copyright © KMD Books
First published in Australia in 2025
by KMD Books
Waikiki, WA 6169

All rights reserved. No part of this book may be used or reproduced by any means, graphic, electronic, or mechanical, including photocopying, recording, taping or by any information storage retrieval system without the written permission of the copyright owner except in the case of brief quotations embodied in critical articles and reviews.

Because of the dynamic nature of the Internet, any web addresses or links contained in this book may have changed since publication and may no longer be vaild. The views expressed in this work are solely those of the author and do not necessarily reflect the views of the publisher and the publisher hereby disclaims any responsibility for them.

 A catalogue record for this work is available from the National Library of Australia

National Library of Australia Catalogue-in-Publication data:
The Beackyard Peace Project Volume One/Cathy Domoney

CONTENTS

ALICE TERRY
COMING TOGETHER WITH LOVE 1

CATHY & SKYE DOMONEY
THE THREADS BETWEEN US 11

GRETCHEN HOLMES, PHD
WHEN IN DOUBT, LOVE YOURSELF HARDER 20

GRIER NEILSON
THROUGH MY LENS 28

JOANNE BROOKS
THE DAY EVERYTHING CHANGED 36

JENNIFER SHARP
BELONGING 46

JUDY MYERS
WHEN DESTINY FINDS YOU 57

DR JULIE DUCHARME
RISING AUTHENTICALLY 67

KAREN PERKS
FINDING PEACE THROUGH STRUGGLE..85

KAREN WEAVER
FINDING YOUR WAY BACK TO INNER PEACE 95

KATHERINE MCLEOD
THE LIFE I CHOSE..109

LAURA MUIRHEAD
WHAT I FOUND IN THE REMAINS 117

LINDA PIERSON
THIS IS WHO I AM IN THE WORLD … 124

MARIE ALESSI
A PIECE OF ME 131

MELANIE RICHARDS
YOU ARE PURE LOVE AND HAPPINESS … 140

NATALIE LEDWELL
THE PRICE OF THE DREAM...146

NICOLE PICCOLO
HOW DID I GET HERE? 154

PAUL BARNAT
FROM BURNOUT TO BREAKTHROUGH 164

PHILIPPA SCOTT
FROM SILENCE TO STRENGTH..170

SANDY FORSTER
THE MAGIC OF MONEY, MINDSET, AND MANIFESTING MILLIONS . 182

SANDRA SPADANUDA
THE GIFT OF HOLDING SPACE 191

SANJA & TOM HENDRICK
FLIPPING THE SCRIPT 201

SCOTT O'MEARA AND BRITTA JENNINGS
FROM TOXIC BONDS TO SOULFUL LOVE 209

SHARON JONES
HEALING FROM WITHIN 219

STEPHANIE VAUGHAN
FINDING STRENGTH THROUGH STYLE 226

VIRGINIE ESPRIT
THREADS OF LOVE 235

DR WENDEL NOORDZIJ
PAWS FOR PEACE 248

ALICE TERRY

COMING TOGETHER WITH LOVE

What does it mean to be a psychic medium, and how can I use that gift to help others and serve the world?

A psychic medium is an individual who has the ability to bring forward evidence of the soul's survival. They are a link between the material and spiritual worlds. A medium hears, sees, smells, tastes and feels spirit vibrations and offers evidence of those passed, delivering their messages of love and guidance.

A medium can possess extra senses; for example:

Feeling – Clairsentient – learn through feelings, clear feeling.

Visual – Clairvoyant – visions and signs, clear seeing.

Thinking – Claircognisant – thoughts of the mind, clear thinking.

Hearing –Clairaudient – auditory sense, clear hearing.

I'm very grateful that these extra senses are as natural as breathing to me. I was born this way, but it has taken years to nurture and evolve that gift into what I am able to do now.

To this day, I still remember being scared to go to bed around age five. It was the early seventies. Patterns had been discovered, and bold was the name of the game. Psychedelic and floral were everywhere: wallpaper, curtains, carpets, upholstery, you name it. Being the youngest, I had to go to bed first – those were the rules. The stairwell light was left on and had to stay on until I was asleep, my curtains had to be pulled properly with no gaps and no drawer or wardrobe door could be left open. My bed was pointed towards the door so I could see if anyone was out on the landing. Once my teddies were all safely tucked in around me, I would pull up the bedcover right up to my nose.

Nothing too outrageous you may think, but *my* world was different. *My* room came alive. The wallpaper had faces, the carpet had animals and the curtains moved as faces morphed in and out. I could smell perfume, baking bread and cigarette smoke even though my parents were non-smokers. I could see shadows in the stairwell coming towards my room. I would firmly reassure all of my teddies that we'd be okay and that I would keep them safe from the 'monsters' all around us. I was terrified of the dark for years.

Though premonitions occurred frequently for me, they were dismissed as an overactive imagination and a bad thing. I was terrified of earthquakes even though Scotland has no significant history of such a thing. (Can I just mention at this point: I moved to New Zealand and lived through the Christchurch earthquakes.)

It was at the age of seven that my gift kicked in. As the youngest of thirteen grandchildren, I was very close to my grandad. He had recently passed but I could still smell his tobacco and hear his voice. But I told no one for years until we were on holiday in England, staying with my aunt. I was ten, the fear of the dark and my overactive imagination were truly freaking my mother out. My aunt, who knew there was something different about me, took me to a spiritual group she went to every week. We were all instructed to close our eyes and see what we could sense. Well, I could see more people than just my grandad. There was and man standing beside a red mini cooper who died in a car crash; a man in a green army uniform, smoking in a fancy hat; and a lady with lots of white hair holding a cat. Within fifteen minutes, I had the whole room in tears. *I could see, hear, feel, and smell dead people.*

Shortly after my grandad passed away, my granny was diagnosed with Alzheimer's, which eventuated in her having to go into a care home. Whilst Mum and my aunt were clearing her home, my grandad spoke loudly in my ear telling me where my gran had hidden her money. After much arguing and frustration from my mum, my aunt finally suggested they humour me, and we found over £300 in the most unusual places. After that my mum was advised by a close family friend to take me to see a famous Scottish clairvoyant named Darlinda, who unfortunately had a two-year waiting list. My premonitions were getting louder. When I was thirteen, my cousin was killed whilst serving in the Special Forces in the Falklands conflict. At his funeral, I could see him in the church sharing our sadness. I was instructed not to tell anyone else what I was seeing or experiencing – we were in a Catholic church.

I was only fifteen by the time our appointment with Darlinda arrived. I was so nervous. What was she going to tell me, what did my future hold, who was I going to marry, what was I going to do for a living? What I was not expecting was for her to tell me in no uncertain terms that I should be at her side of the table and that I was incredibly gifted, the likes of which she had never seen. I had been born with the gift of 'mediumship'. All the other words that were then thrown at me came as a huge relief and, for the very first time, confirmed my belief that I wasn't making it all up. To support me in my development, Darlinda advised me to get a pack of tarot cards as soon as I turned sixteen. My mother reaffirmed that I was to tell no one in our family what I could see or do. 'You'll end up in the looney bin,' she said. After all, half of my family were Catholics and the other half High Church of England, and I was 'conversing with the Devil'.

My tarot cards were the old-fashioned, original type, full of scary pictures – especially the Devil card. No matter how hard I tried to read the book that came with my cards, none of it would stick in my memory. I tried doing a few readings for my mum and friends, but I was confusing myself trying to use the book. I tried using the Celtic Cross style, but everything felt back to front. I then heard a soft and gentle man's voice I had never heard before telling me to put the book down and let the pictures tell the story. My first reading after that reduced my friend into floods of tears as a lovely lady with an Irish accent (her grandmother) – who had passed away with a heart attack, loved lavender and had gifted her a ring – wanted me to tell my friend she was indeed going to be a mother but she just needed a little support (fast-forward to IVF and two children later for her). My mum was still adamant that no one should know.

There is obviously so much more to my card readings now, and of course I have a story of how a new pack of beautiful tarot found me. I have read for thousands of people, and I know that I don't actually need any cards at all but using them makes what I am seeing come alive to my client. The other major learning for me was to ensure that not only was I giving evidence that I was communicating with somebody's loved one but also to convey what they were trying to say. Spirits will provide as much help as they can if allowed to do so. So many mediums I have seen performing are content with bringing evidence of who they have but then cut off the communication. I have always been guided to go that one step further.

So I continued to immerse myself into a world where religion and listening to others was the normal. My gift had been firmly buried in the closet. I kept my premonitions to myself. I was bumbling around thinking I was happy and successful, and as such I never really pushed ahead with who I truly was. I did, however, always have this deep sense that part of me was missing.

During the time my gifts were evolving, I developed asthma after a bad bout of whooping cough. Now, contributors to an asthmatic condition at an energetic level can be: trapped emotion, suffocation and control. I also constantly had earache, sties in my eyes and tonsillitis. I even had glandular fever. At that time, I guessed everyone thought I was just unlucky, but what they didn't know was that not only was I being bullied at school but at home too, hugely supressing who I was. This was the best way to keep me safe, yet my soul was desperate to get my attention. My throat chakra was blocked, my third eye supressed and my imagination closed off and confused – my soul was desperately trying to help me, but I couldn't read the clues back then. My extra senses were growing as fast as I was.

I now know that if I am not listening to my internal guidance, my gift, my guides, the universe – call it what you will – will throw me a significant curveball. Our bodies start to give us significant clues. We all have ailments, and our first step is usually to go to a doctor, whether natural or western, to deal with the consequence, and there is absolutely a place for that. However, when we are not listening to our soul, our physical body feels the disconnection and creates dis-ease that in turn leads to disease. I knew none of this forty years ago, and now that I do, I can pinpoint significant times when life was harder than it needed to be. If I had known how to listen to the clues, things may have been different, but that has also helped me to help others.

One of the most significant times in my life when I was not listening was in 2003. I was high on life in a fast-paced and competitive corporate world when I had cause to visit my doctor. 'Well, Alice,' the doctor said whilst sitting in his office in Stirling, 'you have two choices. You can either go on beta blockers to stop your heart palpitations and talk to a counsellor, *or* you could leave your job.' Suddenly I felt that I was free; it was my health or my early death!

My palpations stopped. I had given up my stressful sales job full of bullies and competitive egos and taken some time to balance myself, but I had also begun to consider stepping back into the corporate world (clearly not listening fully to my inner being), prompting another curveball. I was unexpectedly pregnant and at the end of my pregnancy in 2004, my son was found to be a transverse lie, resulting in an emergency caesarean. This was a big shock, especially when I had expected to have the full birthing experience. During this procedure my blood pressure crashed with the drugs, and I was very ill. I did not get the opportunity to bond to my baby as much as I thought I would. I was spiralling into postnatal depression.

So there I am again, back at the doctor being told I could have Prozac or talk to a psychologist. Now, given my unusual set of skills, I opted for a spiritual psychologist, who would finally support me in embracing my extra senses and set me free from my closet to step into who I was born to be. When life is proving too hard and you are trying to fix it and control every little thing as I was, your soul will upset your apple cart and your health can suffer. Paying attention to your body and listening to your soul is a wonderful way to start your healing process. I had to go through this and other things to learn how to help others navigate their way.

This huge amount of learning and realisation has enabled me to develop something I call an 'energy reset'. This enables me, from a current 'selfie' to draw a person's energy and identify significant things that are going on for them in their life – including things that there is no way they could possibly know. I remember advising one client who had been ill after travelling abroad that she actually had undiagnosed parasites. She had been aimlessly trying to live her life with a debilitating condition for months. Energy resets have also been particularly useful for parents who are at a loss with their children as my mum was with me.

It was at the age of thirty-seven that I was finally ready to embrace my true calling. All the right people, at the right time, aligned with me and I have never looked back. I was finally in my flow. I'm often asked how I shut it off, and the truth is I can't as it is just who I am. What I have learnt through experience – which has been my life learning and still is my life learning – is that the information I receive is not mine to keep and I have to pass it on. I remember once, visiting Canterbury Cathedral, there was a woman sitting all alone hunched in a front pew, grief stricken … except that she wasn't alone at all as she had the spirits of two men sat either side of her: her husband and her son. I still regret to this day not having the courage to speak to this woman as I may have been able to ease her pain in some small way.

This is particularly true when I am performing live in front of an audience. How does it work? When I'm preparing for a live evening show, my body usually stops me eating at around 2pm. This happens so that I am not too grounded, digesting food. I start to find it hard to concentrate on everyday tasks, external noises are extremely loud and smells make me feel nauseous. I then begin to see spirits (the audience's loved ones lining up in my head, like a bus trip outing) and usually hear a name, and I know that this is the first person I will connect with that evening. When I get to the venue, I have to be away from everyone beforehand until showtime. I start to see light bulbs, like constellations, of where spirits are standing in the audience like a guidance map for me so that I know where to go. When I am live, there is a strong energetic pull to where that light bulb is, and just like that I feel the person standing with me, very much like Whoopi Goldberg in the movie *Ghost* – I know the gender first, then how tall, how they held themselves, then the personality pops in. It's important to bring the evidence, the personal details that make you laugh, cry or bring you comfort. Lastly comes the message.

One of the most memorable was when I brought through a young girl who was the daughter of a lady in the front row. This young girl was joking around, showing me she was flicking a light switch on and off. 'On, off, on, off,' she said several times. The lady in the front row broke down because she had had the responsibility of switching off her daughter's life support machine. Her daughter conveyed that she was fine and didn't blame her mum in any way, which freed her mum of the massive debilitating guilt she was carrying for having to make that decision. Needless to say, the healing was huge.

So from the child frightened of the dark, I now step into my light every day, offering readings, energy resets, soul alignments, workshops and finally creating my own cards that will ignite everyone's amazing imagination. I do so for people around the world and from all walks of life, supporting them with closure and comfort from a loved one's passing or guiding them on their next steps in their life's journey. Gifted with all my extra senses, I made it my mission to bring Mediumship into the twenty-first century. I am grateful to all of the thousands of people I have helped and guided over the years, and I am grateful to my soul for shouting so loud I had no choice but to listen. Also, I am so grateful to all of my guides, all of my loved ones and all your loved ones who continue to communicate with me, reminding me that the two worlds can exist and that they really do come together with love.

ABOUT ALICE

Alice Terry is a medium of the highest order. She has an extraordinary gift but has not lost sight of the fact that she is also an everyday working mum. Born in Scotland, she became aware of her gift at the age of seven and has evolved that gift into how she works today. Alice works a little differently to most people, but it is her heart and authenticity that people love and respond to. Spending any time with Alice is a unique experience – being in the company of someone who sees directly into your soul is both enlightening and uplifting.

Alice is based in South Australia and uses her extraordinary mediumship gift to engage with audiences worldwide, helping people in so many ways, whether through grief and loss, lack of direction or pure counselling, enabling you to find clarity in your life.

Alice is available for personal readings, regression therapy, energy resets (TM ATerry), learning workshops, soul energy alignments (TM ATerry) and public speaking.

Alice provides a source of inspiration to everyone she meets every day, following her calling of bringing two worlds together: 'coming together with love'.

Her own set of oracle cards, the most unique and individual to hit the

ALICE TERRY

market, are due to be released for Christmas 2025

aliceterry.com
aliceterrywallofremembrance.com
Facebook & Instagram: International Psychic Medium Alice Terry
Email: alice@aliceterry.com

CATHY & SKYE DOMONEY

THE THREADS BETWEEN US
THE MOTHER'S OPENING REFLECTION

There are few relationships as layered, complex, fragile and strong as that between a mother and her daughter. When I became a mother, I promised myself that the trauma and hardships I had endured in my own childhood would *end with me*. I was determined that my daughters and sons would not carry the weight of the wounds I had been handed.

For years, I worked tirelessly on my own healing, on therapy, on personal growth, on consciously choosing new patterns. I told myself, *If I can be aware, if I can do the inner work, if I can make different choices, then the pain will not trickle down into the next generation.*

But what I learned, many years later, sitting across from my adult daughter Skye, is that despite all of my effort, some things did filter through. Not because I wasn't careful, not because I didn't love fiercely, but because I am human.

This is the story of our conversation, an unflinching, vulnerable dialogue between mother and daughter about trauma, honesty, mistakes, forgiveness and love.

WITNESSING WITHOUT WORDS (SKYE'S VOICE)

When I was little, Mum never sat me down and never told me, 'I'm unhappy with my body,' or 'I need to lose weight.' She never once criticised my appearance or compared me to anyone else. She always spoke to me in the language of empowerment, telling me I was beautiful, capable, strong and worthy.

And yet, I absorbed something unspoken.

I remember the kitchen table, covered with stacks of weight-loss books. I remember seeing the Weight Watchers materials, the food diaries and the counting and measuring. I remember Mum leaving the house to attend meetings.

At the time, I didn't fully understand it. I was young, too young to interpret what dieting meant. But the images seared into my memory. Years later, when I struggled with food myself, those images resurfaced.

It wasn't that she *told* me I should shrink myself. It was when I watched her trying so hard to shrink herself. Children notice everything. Even when we don't have the words, even when parents believe they are protecting us, we are absorbing and interpreting the world around us.

THE WEIGHT OF THE UNSEEN

When I stopped eating as a teenager, Mum was devastated. She asked herself a thousand questions: *Was it me? Did I do this? Did she learn it from me?*

The truth is complicated. Yes, I had internalised some of what I saw at home. But I was also swimming in a culture that glorified thinness. My peers at school were talking about diets. Social media bombarded me with images of unattainable beauty. Magazines, billboards and television all reinforced the messages that our worth as women was tied to the size of our bodies.

Mum could control the words spoken inside our home, but she couldn't control the conversations in the schoolyard, the adverts on the street or the endless stream of cultural expectations.

Looking back now, I see how impossible it was for her to shield me from it all. And I see how much guilt she carried in believing that she should have been able to.

THE BACKYARD PEACE PROJECT: VOL 1

PARENTING WHILE HEALING

One of the hardest truths to face as a child is realising that your parents are not finished products. They are human beings still on their own journey.

My mum spent much of my childhood working through her own trauma. She was determined that the pain she had endured would not pass to her children. But as she was processing, I was watching.

She didn't sit me down and pour out her struggles in detail, but I witnessed the signs: the stress, the exhaustion, the times when she was overwhelmed. Those images, too, became part of my subconscious.

When you're a child, you don't have the capacity to separate what belongs to you from what belongs to your parent. You just absorb. You carry. You interpret.

That is the complexity of parenting while healing. You can be the most conscious parent in the world and still, simply by existing in your own humanity, pass on fragments of your struggle.

THE HARD CONVERSATIONS (CATHY'S VOICE)

When Skye first shared with me what she had carried, it was like a punch to the heart. I had worked so hard to protect her. I had spent years intentionally choosing different ways, reading books, attending courses, doing the work on myself so that my children wouldn't have to carry my pain.

And yet, here she was, telling me that some of it had still seeped through.

It was hard to receive. I felt waves of guilt, sadness and grief. But beneath that pain, I also felt gratitude. Gratitude that she trusted me enough to speak her truth. Grateful that our relationship was strong enough to hold the weight of it.

Because here's the truth: parents will always make mistakes. No amount of awareness or effort will make you perfect. The question is not whether you will falter, but whether you will *own it*.

THE POWER OF OWNERSHIP

There were moments in my parenting that I wish I could redo. Times when I was overwhelmed, when I snapped, when I couldn't show up the way I wanted to.

Later, when I gained perspective, I would go back to Skye and say, 'I am sorry. I didn't show up for you the way you needed in that moment.' Sometimes she didn't even remember the incident until I reminded her. But the act of acknowledgement mattered.

I have met many adults who still carry wounds from their childhood, not because their parents made mistakes, but because their parents *denied them*. They were gaslit, dismissed or told they were imagining things. The wound was deepened not by the mistake itself, but by the refusal to admit it.

Skye has told me herself: if I had denied, if I had refused to acknowledge, if I had tried to preserve an image of myself as the 'perfect mother', she would have drifted away. Our closeness would have eroded.

It wasn't the mistakes that fractured relationships – it was the silence, the denial, the pretending.

LEARNING RADICAL COMMUNICATION

One of the things that has kept our bond strong is what we now call 'radical communication'.

We don't shy away from uncomfortable conversations, but we also honour timing. Sometimes Skye will say, 'Mum, I need to give you some hard feedback. Are you ready to receive it?' And sometimes, I will say,

'Not right now. I'm too tired, too stressed. But I want to hear you. Can we revisit this when I can respond with balance?'

This structure gives us both safety. It means the conversation isn't avoided, it's simply postponed until it can be fruitful.

We also learned the importance of intention. Before a hard conversation, we ask ourselves: *What do I want to get out of this?* If the goal is to strengthen the relationship, then even criticism can be offered in love.

MOVING OUT: A NEW PERSPECTIVE (SKYE'S VOICE)

At the start of this year, I moved out of my childhood home for the first time. It was a huge shift, after spending nearly every waking moment of my life in close connection with Mum.

Being apart gave me space to reflect. I started to see my childhood through new eyes, not just as the child living it, but as an adult looking back. I realised how much Mum had prepared me, not by making me a replica of her, but by giving me the tools to be my own person.

She never tried to live her life through me. She never demanded that I follow her exact path. She gave me feedback, yes, but always from the perspective of, 'This is my view. You are your own person. It is your decision.'

That freedom has been priceless. It means that even when I make mistakes now, I don't feel crushed by them. They are learning curves. And I know I can go back to Mum, not to be told 'I told you so', but to be asked, 'What would you like to do differently next time?'

LESSONS FOR PARENTS AND CHILDREN

From our journey, we've drawn some lessons that we hope will help others:
- **Allow yourself to be human.** Parents are not perfect. Children are

not perfect. Be kind to yourself.
- **Receive criticism as love.** When your child brings you something hard, it's not to tear you down; it's usually a plea to stay close.
- **Be transparent.** Acknowledge mistakes. Apologise. Own your humanity.
- **Respect timing.** Hard conversations land best when both people are resourced and ready.
- **Stay curious.** Ask, 'What is my child experiencing? What is it like for them right now?' instead of only reacting to behaviour.
- **Encourage individuality.** Let your children be themselves, not extensions of you.

A LETTER FROM DAUGHTER TO MOTHER

Dear Mum,

I want you to know that despite the challenges, I wouldn't change you for the world. You showed me what it looks like to face your trauma and not run from it. You showed me resilience, even in the moments when you thought you were failing.

Yes, I witnessed things, your dieting, your overwhelm, your pain, but I also witnessed your love, your strength and your willingness to own your mistakes. That ownership is what made all the difference. It kept me close when I might have drifted.

Thank you for empowering me, even when you were still finding your own empowerment. Thank you for never trying to mould me into your image but instead giving me the freedom to be myself. Thank you for creating a home where truth could be spoken, even when it hurt.

I am who I am because of you, not in spite of your struggles, but partly because of how you chose to face them. I love you.

Always,

Skye

THE BACKYARD PEACE PROJECT: VOL 1

A LETTER FROM MOTHER TO DAUGHTER

My dearest Skye,

Reading your words, I am both humbled and grateful. As a mother, my deepest wish was always that you would grow into a confident, resilient, compassionate woman who could stand in her own power. And here you are, proving every day that you have done exactly that.

I know there were times I didn't show up the way you needed me to. Times when my own overwhelm spilled into my parenting. I wish I could go back and give you more calm, more ease, more steadiness. But what consoles me is knowing that even in those moments, our love and honesty kept us close.

Thank you for trusting me enough to share your truth. Thank you for reminding me that parenting is not about perfection, but about connection. Thank you for teaching me that vulnerability goes both ways, that a child can teach a mother just as much as a mother teaches a child.

I am endlessly proud of you, not just for what you do, but for who you are. You are thoughtful, brave and compassionate. You are your own person, and that fills me with joy.

I will always be here, not as a perfect mother, but as your mother, who loves you beyond measure.

All my love,
Mama. x

By making peace with our struggles as parents, we learn to extend that same compassion to the mistakes our parents made, giving us the chance to share forgiveness and love with them. Hopefully, they will still be here to feel the warmth of that love and the healing it brings.

ABOUT CATHY & SKYE

CATHY

Cathy Domoney is an internationally recognised transformational coach, author and changemaker whose life's work is dedicated to dissolving barriers to human potential. With over twenty years of experience and advanced training in trauma-informed practice, Cathy has guided leaders, executives and entrepreneurs to achieve breakthroughs both personally and professionally.

She is the Founder and CEO of The Backyard Peace Project (BYPP), a global movement creating ripples of peace through ambassador networks, youth initiatives and powerful anthologies. Her vision is to inspire collective healing and connection, starting in local communities and expanding worldwide.

Cathy also serves as chair of the Association of Transformational Leaders, Australia, where she brings together pioneers of influence to model authentic, heart-centred leadership and holds a leadership position for She Talks, Australia Division. She has collaborated with global icons including Jack Canfield, Montel Williams and Natalie Ledwell, and was recognised as a Women Changing the World Awards 2024 finalist for her impact in leadership and social change.

Her private coaching practice attracts high-achieving professionals and entrepreneurs who seek radical breakthroughs. Cathy is renowned for her honesty, depth and ability to dissolve stress, burnout and subconscious blocks, enabling her clients to achieve record-breaking success while reclaiming balance and peace.

Beyond her professional achievements, Cathy is a devoted wife of thirty years and mother to five neurodiverse children. Her journey of resilience and compassion fuels her mission: to help others rise above struggle, embrace their innate power, and create legacies of love, impact and peace.

cathydomoney.com
thebackyardpeaceproject.com
cathydomoney@gmail.com
Facebook | Instagram | TikTok | Linkedin: @cathydomoney

SKYE

Skye is a visionary creative who delves into and explores various media, which inspires her creative projects. With a flair for storytelling and a naturally bubbly personality, she channels warmth and energy into everything she creates – whether it's through vibrant art, imaginative worlds or content designed to make people smile. Passionate about connection and creativity, Skye thrives on crafting experiences that spark inspiration and unites others.

GRETCHEN HOLMES, PHD
WHEN IN DOUBT, LOVE YOURSELF HARDER

When I was a little girl, food was my refuge. Throughout my life, it was my comfort, my peace, my best friend … until it wasn't.

I was an overweight child who grew up to be an overweight adult and then a morbidly obese adult. It's a battle I've fought my entire life. I learned at an early age that no matter what was wrong, food made me feel better. At least for the moment. Self-soothing with food was my coping mechanism. After all, you can only feel so sad, angry, uncertain, guilty, embarrassed or whatever the emotion, for so long before you need to make yourself feel better, right? That certainly was the case for me growing up.

I grew up in an alcoholic home, and that meant a lot of uncertainty, fear, anger and sadness. To be fair, there was a lot of love, too, but there was significant dysfunction, as there often is when there is addiction. I was the middle child, the only girl, and I felt invisible. Why? Not just because I was the middle child, but because I didn't have anything wrong with me to compete for attention.

My older brother was a hemophiliac, which meant he was frequently in the hospital for serious health issues. My other brother, six years younger, was hit by a truck while riding his bicycle on a country road when he was eight years old. He was in critical condition for a long time, and we weren't sure he was going to survive. We all spent a lot of time at the hospital. And then there was my dad. My dad had a lot of demons. He wasn't as easy to love, but we loved him, and he loved us. He had a tough time showing it, though.

During his active drinking days, the house was filled with chaos. We often didn't know if Dad was going to come home after work, especially on payday. Sometimes he was gone for days, sometimes for more than a week or two. Sooner or later, he would come home. There would be arguments, he would stop drinking for a while, but he always started up again. Sleep was constantly interrupted, we never knew what kind of mood he would be in if he was home, and after a while, we hoped he wouldn't come home at all. Then we felt guilty about it. The stress was becoming too much. Mom did her best to stabilise things, but she had her hands full. She worked full-time, which meant taking care of my younger brother, and the house fell to me (not unusual in those days).

My dad was a shift worker for most of his life and was often onnights. Thus, it wasn't unusual during the more unbearable times that Mom would pack up our things in garbage bags in the middle of the night, and we all would go stay with relatives. The pattern would repeat for years. I was embarrassed. I felt shame. I was angry. So, I ate.

If you grew up in or are experiencing addiction in your home, none of this is surprising. We all have our war stories. Over time, growing up in a dysfunctional home does a number on your self-worth, how you see yourself, and how you talk to yourself to make sense of your experiences. It also means we spend most of our time in survival mode, hyper-focused on reading the room and picking up on cues to make sure we are ready for whatever comes next. Being in survival mode, even as a young child, I was always waiting for the next crisis. And I was always eating.

I knew I was bigger than my friends; if I hadn't realised this, the taunts and teasing would have clued me in. I would try to lose weight, and I would lose a few pounds, but then I would stop trying, start listening to the negative comments from others, and stop trying. Then, I would beat myself up for failing, gain weight, and the pattern would start all over again.

Over time, I perfected beating myself up and tearing myself down before anyone else could. After a while, it became my go-to behavior, especially if I was struggling. Over the years, I realised it wasn't what I said out loud that was the biggest problem; after all, my attempt at self-deprecating humor was an effective defense mechanism. If I insulted myself first, it disarmed them, took away their power. The most damaging behaviour was what I was saying to myself.

In 2021, I was diagnosed diabetic. I was devastated. I was already a three-time cancer survivor and over 100lb overweight. My health was declining, and I was constantly losing the battle with my weight. Like many, I fell into a cycle of starting a new weightloss program, having a little success (or sometimes a lot), losing my footing, quitting, gaining the weight back, and then beating myself up for it. I did this for decades.

I didn't realise until I had successfully lost over 100lb, kept it off for three years, and then started to gain some back, how toxic my relationship with myself had become.

How that the very time I needed to be my own cheerleader, my most ardent supporter, I was anything but that. I immediately fell back into old habits: shame, embarrassment, self-loathing and disgust.

When I finally realised that what I was telling myself was defining my life, not what anyone else was telling me. That was a powerful moment. I realised that I had the power, not anyone else. What I had been doing, I finally understood, was relinquishing my power to other people to avoid uncomfortable situations, conflict and to people-please.

Once you become aware of these things, you can't unknow them. So, I had to figure out a way forward that would support my life, my dreams and my goals, and now I knew the path forward was not through loving myself less.

When we stumble or fall, it can be embarrassing. It's a human response to an uncomfortable situation. However, it's also an opportunity to learn, to grow and to change what needs changing. The problem isn't the fact that we feel bad when that happens; the problem occurs when we stay stuck in a mindset that doesn't allow us to learn, grow or change from the event. The problem gets exacerbated when we turn on ourselves so harshly that we make it almost impossible to rise above the noise and the negativity.

There's a better way forward: When you stumble or fall, instead of beating yourself up and succumbing to shame and embarrassment, try loving yourself harder. I know it's counterintuitive, but has all of the self-loathing and beating yourself up over the years ever really helped? Has telling yourself you couldn't do something, that you're not worthy of a good life, ever propelled you forward? Has talking to yourself this way ever given you the confidence to attack your goals with energy and vitality? No? Me, neither.

Loving yourself harder through difficult times takes practice. It requires intentionality. It requires patience and grace for yourself. Those old habits have probably been there for a long time, so it may take a while to shift your mindset, but it's worth it. After all, life is hard enough when others tell us we can't do something or achieve a goal; we don't have to chime in with the same tired message. This doesn't mean we don't hold ourselves accountable, we must. However, we can do it with self-compassion and grace. They can exist side-by-side.

Here are some ways you can start shifting your mindset to a place of self-love: Observe how you talk to yourself. When you make a mistake, what do you say to yourself (either out loud or in your head)? Do you tell yourself that people make mistakes sometimes, learn from them and then move on, or do you automatically berate yourself? I've learned to intentionally ask myself what I would say to a friend if they made the same mistake. Is that the tone I would use? Are those the words I would use?

If not, what should I be saying to myself?

Identify your self-limiting beliefs. What do you say to yourself when an opportunity arises? Do you automatically talk your way out of it before considering it? Do you automatically tell yourself you're not smart enough, attractive enough, deserving enough? If so, those are some pretty powerful self-limiting beliefs. We all have them; the key is to first identify them (which can be tricky since we take it for granted that *they're true*) and then ask yourself, *Is this true? Am I really not smart enough? Where did that even come from?* Even if something was true when we were younger, it doesn't mean it still is. Maybe we were not very coordinated when we were growing up, so we decided (or someone told us) that we weren't athletic. Is that still true? Really? Question everything you tell yourself. It's important to debunk those limiting beliefs.

Engage in actions that support you and your goals. Changing how we talk to ourselves is critical, but followed up with action? Well, that's powerful. Trying to get healthy? Identify actions or activities that you can do that help support your goals. My health journey is important to me, so I want to continue to reinforce to myself and others that it's a priority. That's why every Sunday afternoon, I prepare my lunches and meals for the week. I learned a long time ago that I don't do well when I have to make decisions on the go; I need to have my meals healthy and accessible, or there's a good chance I won't make healthy choices. I may not always have control of situations, but the ones I do, I want to be prepared.

Preparing my meals does two things: One, it sets me up for success for the week.

That's always a win. Two, and this is probably most important, it reinforces through action to myself and others, that I'm worth focusing on my needs, not only through words but through action.

Normalise asking for help. One of the most profound ways you can love yourself is to ask for help when you need it. We know that it can be embarrassing, that sometimes we feel shame, but nothing exhibits self-love more than asking for help when you need it.

Many of us are givers. We support others, no questions asked. We put ourselves last automatically, but what is important to consider is that we also need to learn how to receive. We need to learn how to accept help with grace, humility and gratitude. When we allow ourselves to be vulnerable, admit we don't have all of the answers and realise we were never supposed to know everything in the first place, that's when we are the most human. When we reach out to others, while uncomfortable at first, it is empowering.

It is a powerful action that reinforces that we are worth others' time and effort, and we deserve to invest in ourselves.

I wanted to hide when I gained some weight back. I was embarrassed. After all, I had published a book about my transformational journey and had a podcast. I should have known better, I told myself. But here's the thing, while I learned a lot about myself during my weightloss journey, through the help of a coach and a therapist, I learned a whole lot more during the last year as I struggled with my weight. I learned that I am always susceptible to falling back into old habits. I learned that I didn't have all the answers; I hadn't figured it all out. I learned I needed help once again.

In my book and on my podcast, I talk a lot about loving ourselves through the hard times, especially through the hard times. After struggling for almost a year, I realized I *had to walk the walk*. I asked myself, *What would you advise a friend to do if they were struggling with their weight? I knew I would say, Find some help. You don't always have to do everything on your own.* It's easier to recognise that others need help than ourselves, but we have to get better at normalising asking for help. I believe not asking for help punishes us and reinforces the belief that we aren't worthy to live a robust life.

There is zero shame in asking for help when you're struggling. The question is, how far down the rabbit hole do we want to go before we ask for help? I decided I had gone far enough, so I made a phone call. Best decision ever.

We all struggle with something. We all stumble, and sometimes we fall. Instead of responding to it the same old way, I challenge you to try something different: I challenge you to love yourself harder when the instinct is to do the opposite. This will allow you the space to embrace all that is special about you and realise that you are amazing and unique and enough already. In fact, I suspect you are more than enough. Celebrate that.

ABOUT GRETCHEN

A three-time cancer survivor, Gretchen Holmes is a dynamic speaker, author and host of *The Work in Between* podcast, where she and her guests take a deep dive into the struggles, joys and daily actions that move us towards physical, emotional and spiritual health. Diagnosed with diabetes in 2021, Gretchen transformed her life by losing over 100lb and continues to focus on the daily work necessary to maintain a vibrant, healthy lifestyle. Previously, Gretchen worked as a stand-up comedian and continues to use humour to navigate the complexities of life. She was also co-creator, co-producer, writer and on-air talent for WUMR's *Let's Talk Health* and was named as one of 100 Successful Women to Know on the Gulf Coast in 2022 by *Gulf Coast Woman* magazine. Her book, *The Work in Between: A Memoir* about stepping out of my shadows, is available now.

gretchenholmesphd.com

GRIER NEILSON
THROUGH MY LENS

I never in my wildest dreams thought I would be featured in the media, in my underwear, during my fiftieth lap around the sun.

Yet here I am, encouraging, empowering and inspiring women fifty and over to be seen.

Hi, I'm Grier Neilson. An alchemist photographer. An intimate artist. A make-up artist, a body painter, an artisan. I'm an adventurer, an ocean dreamer, a cyclist, a yogi, a paddle boarder, a beach bum, an amateur sailor, a traveller. I'm a nature lover, a boho soul, a mum, a partner, a daughter, a stepdaughter, a sister, an auntie and a friend. I've been a skydiver, a race car driver, a triathlete, and I am so much more than all of these.

At the core of everything I do is a simple truth: my purpose is to help people to tell their authentic stories, which at times can be lifesaving. It's about feeling safe enough to share the true you, for example, sharing the scars of deep wounds or showing the multiple equipment you need to survive through your disability, not keeping it hidden. I love what I've done, where I've come from and who I've become.

In the year leading up to my fiftieth lap around the sun, something came into sharp focus: Women over fifty are the least photographed demographic in the world. That broke my heart. I knew I wanted to change this narrative. So, to celebrate turning fifty, I made it my mission to photograph myself and forty-nine other women in their fifties, and in doing so, raise the bar on how we see and celebrate ourselves.

THE BACKYARD PEACE PROJECT: VOL 1

The more women I spoke to, the more stories I heard of invisibility. Women feeling irrelevant, overlooked. Statistics back it up, homelessness rises sharply for women over fifty, and suicide rates climb. I heard stories of women whose confidence had slowly eroded, who felt lost after decades of nurturing others, or who no longer saw themselves as beautiful, desirable or worthy.

I've resonated with some of these things, too, in different waves of life.

For me, the journey of not feeling seen began when I was a child. My parents divorced when I was six, my younger brother and I lived with my mum and grandparents, and saw my dad fortnightly on weekends. My family on both sides were loving and extremely talented creatives, painters, drawers, artists, sign writers, craftspeople.

But despite my heartfelt passion, I couldn't draw, paint or write like they could; dyslexia was a part of life, and I learned to dim myself, quietly believing I wasn't as talented or capable, only a little bit creative, just good enough. I carried myself with such strength that no one realised how much I was dimming myself inside. And in love, too, I often felt unseen — from my teenage years, up till my marriage and then after divorce. I was always searching for connection, yet even in intimacy, I wasn't always truly visible. I was loved for my strength, but rarely for my vulnerability. And the strange irony was that I often drew attention, sometimes more than I wanted, and still, I wasn't truly seen?"

My journey towards my passion for photography started around the age of twelve when for the first time ever I won a prize. Little did I know it would be so significant in shaping my career. It was a little gold Kodak Disc 3100 camera. It had a disc-shaped negative, and it was magic. Over time I bought my self an SLR and began to photograph nature, landscapes and marco work. These images became gifts for the family. A few short TAFE courses followed, but mostly, I taught myself through passion, experimentation and sheer persistence.

I'd heard the old saying: 'Don't turn your hobby into a career, you'll grow to dislike it.' So, at nineteen, I worked behind the scenes... in a photographic studio and became a make-up artist to stay close to the creative energy. When I moved to Queensland I would use my camera to create fun and memorable Christmas cards with my dog and I body-painted my kids. I was a freelance make-up artist with published work. Eventually, I picked up my camera to photograph the pregnant woman and cancer survivors I was body painting; this work lit something up in me.

As a young mum I produced two memorable calendars: one with the Townsville Dragon Boat Club 'Twin Titties', and one with Friends of the Birth Centre. Not only did I do the body painting, design and the photography. I did the make-up, the hair and shared the art direction and production. These projects weren't just creative, they were life-changing. They raised funds and told stories of survival, motherhood and strength. I'll never forget the people I met. And I'll never forget the impact those experiences had on my clients, their families and me.

During this time, I went through one of the most devastating periods of my life. My marriage fell apart. My ex-husband, an officer in the army, was living with post-traumatic stress disorder, PTSD. It was a very dark time, one that without my kids, I don't know what door I would have opened. That alone is a whole book in itself, but what I can say is that the ripple effects of his trauma impacted every corner of our lives. I had a newborn and a six-year-old when we separated.

I moved back to Adelaide, thinking it would be temporary. But everything changed: my lifestyle, my identity, my sense of self. The creative part of me went quiet. I was cut off financially, suddenly on the edge of homelessness, with two young children and no stable income.

Through the separation and divorce, I just kept going. I fought for what I believed in. I put my kids first. I did what so many women do in crisis: I survived. My two kids, my dog and I lived in a one-bedroom flat behind my mum's place. It was cramped, humbling and exhausting and was one of the hardest times in my life. Mission Australia helped me until I could stand on my own feet again.

Consequently, my creative spark lay dormant for years. I focused on cycling and running to stay grounded. I was a single mum, doing my best. But at one point, I found myself considering surgery, a tummy tuck and breast implants. I wanted to find that connection, love and believed no-one would want me as I was. Two kids, no boobs, sagging skin. As I sat with the surgeon, something clicked.

What am I doing?

I didn't want surgery, I wanted experiences. So instead, I gave myself a divorce present. A month overseas. A trip of a lifetime to France, the UK and Amsterdam, I cycled with a group of friends alongside the Tour de France and climbed massive mountains. Ohh, did I feel empowered and strong and new, I could do anything, it changed me. I came back lit up from the inside.

When I launched Flock50, I wanted to make women over fifty visible. I discovered that many had never been photographed professionally. Some had always been behind the camera, others felt undesirable or lost going through perimenopause or after menopause. Some had given decades to raising children, while others felt lonely, others felt faded in their careers or disconnected in their marriages. Some had endured the trauma of abuse, losing siblings, parents and children, and carried grief in silence. Many were left lost or had gone through major surgeries or near-death experiences. Some had lived a fabulous life of love and laughter and wanted to celebrate all that life had gifted them, some to surely inspire and feel empowered. There is no wrong or right, it is about your story and what makes you uniquely you.

Flock50 is about disrupting that narrative. It's a movement for change. It's about women being seen by themselves and, in turn, by others. It's about reclaiming our voice, our sensuality, our power, our stories, our confidence and letting go of the hefty and unnecessary weight of the opinions of others.

I couldn't ask these fifty women to step into vulnerability if I wasn't willing to do the same. So, I led by example.

I packed a suitcase and went to a little B&B and photographed myself. In my underwear. Some nude with a guitar, some in a fluffy jacket on a bed. You could see my baby skin, my tattoos, my jewellery, my essence. Sitting by the fire that night, I flipped through the back of my camera and tears welled up.

I felt proud. I felt at home. I fell in love with myself again.

That night, I shared a reel of those photos on social media. It went wild. I had no idea that one of those images would be featured across Australia on national TV, *The Morning Show*.

That it would be printed nearly full-page in The Advertiser on the day of the Flock50 exhibition and book launch – 3 August 2024.

My daughter was with me at the launch, but I texted my sixteen-year-old son: Hey, babe, just a heads up, there's a photo of me in my underwear in The Advertiser today. He replied,

Yeah, I know. People at lacrosse are talking about it. (LOL.) He wasn't phased. I've always tried to model body positivity in our home, nudie runs, laughter, no shame. I never hid from my kids, never shamed myself. I wanted them to feel at home in their skin.

Being a role model to them and to others has always been important to me. I love to inspire.

Photographing fifty women in one project has been the most rewarding experience of my career. To have them open their hearts, trust me with their stories and allow me to capture them authentically, it's an honour.

As an alchemist photographer, I don't just take pictures. I help women celebrate themselves. I hold space for healing. I create images that capture who they are, who they've been and who they're becoming. Whether they want to feel sexy, wise, sensual, bold, playful or soft, I help bring that out.

This isn't about documenting the whole family, the holiday or the business. It's about you, your essence, your story, your legacy.

Bringing it all together in a book and an exhibition, where these women are celebrated, regardless of background, size, story or status, has been my life's work.

Each edition of Flock50 evolves, and each edition holds a collaboration of over 2,500 years of collective wisdom, self-love and fierce feminine power.

So let me say this: be photographed.

Whether by someone else or through self-portraiture, it is powerful. It's a healing journey.

Seeing yourself, truly seeing yourself, can help you come home.

Print the photos. Hold them in your hands. Share them. Honour yourself.

Because I see you.

ABOUT GRIER

Grier is the founder and visionary behind Bohemian Ekko Creative, an artist with a passionate and unconventional approach to capturing the beauty and authenticity of women. With over thirty years of experience in the realms of beauty, make-up artistry, body painting, photography and stage wardrobe, Grier's artistry is deeply rooted in her love for storytelling, individuality and connection. Her business name, Bohemian Ekko, reflects her creative philosophy: 'Bohemian' captures her free-spirited, unconventional style, while 'Ekko' represents the timeless memory that each image echoes, preserving it for future generations.

Throughout her career, Grier has worked with clients ranging from everyday individuals to global brands, including The Berlin Opera, Sony Picture Releasing and Universal Pictures, and she has collaborated alongside renowned personalities like Pink, Hugh Jackman, Taylor Swift, Bryan Brown and Miranda Tapsell. Her commercial talent work recently took her to the other side of the camera for the SA Tourism commercial 'Travel. Our Way'.

Despite her broad industry experience, her focus remains consistent: to create authentic connections and a safe, welcoming space for each client. Grier's passion lies in helping women see themselves as they are

THE BACKYARD PEACE PROJECT: VOL 1

— unfiltered, empowered, and beautiful. Her recent Flock50 project, an exhibition and coffee table book featuring portraits of fifty women in their fifties, showcases women as they are, each one stepping into courage and leaving behind self-doubt. This project isn't just a collection of photographs; it's a movement of self-acceptance that addresses the experience of women who often feel unseen as they age. By curating over 2,500 years of collective wisdom, Flock50 captures the vulnerability, strength and depth of each woman, challenging social norms and celebrating each phase of life.

In addition to Flock50, Grier's 'Feathered' retreat invites women to step into their femininity, shedding societal expectations in favour of self-expression through art. Integrating the rugged Australian landscape with the naked female form, Feathered produces evocative, nature-based art that serves as both a personal journey and a keepsake.

Throughout her work, Grier witnesses the transformative power of seeing oneself through a compassionate lens, one that celebrates the journey, scars and stories that make each person unique. Her approach to photography is deeply personal, providing each client with an experience that captures their essence while fostering self-acceptance and love. Grier's ultimate goal is to shift the way women perceive themselves, not only for their own empowerment but also to influence generations to come.

Bohemian Ekko Creative, now in its thirteenth year, stands as a testament to Grier's dedication to her craft and her clients. Each image is more than a photograph; it's a reflection, a memory and an echo of the individual's true self. For Grier, the work she does is not only about capturing moments but about creating a legacy of empowerment, authenticity and lasting self-love.

bohemianekko.com

JOANNE BROOKS
THE DAY EVERYTHING CHANGED

September 2000, after seventeen years of marriage, my world cracked wide open.

Two police officers walked into my office. 'Are you Mrs Ashton?' they asked.

We stepped into a small room. One of them looked me in the eye and said the words that split my life in two:

'Your husband has been killed in a car accident.'

At first, that's all I knew. It was blunt. Shocking. Final.

What I didn't know in that moment was that a coronial inquest would later rule his death a suicide. Another layer of trauma I hadn't seen coming, and one that reshaped how I looked back on everything we'd lived through together.

Shock. Silence. And then the next question that felt like another blow:

'Where is your daughter?'

I was in no position to do anything. Somebody rang the day care on my behalf and, thank goodness, Nicole was safe.

Within twenty-four hours, my doctor came to see me. I'll never forget the look on his face – heavy, awkward, almost apologetic. He told me my husband was HIV-positive. Another truth I hadn't been told. Another secret kept in silence.

I didn't even have time to grieve one trauma before the next hit.

And then came the funeral. His family told me flat-out: 'You will not speak.'

So I didn't. I stayed quiet. I agreed. I didn't rock the boat. It's what I had always done.

But the pressure didn't stop. They started telling me I had to move back to where they were, that it was best for Nicole, and that I should do what they wanted.

For the first time in my thirty-eight years, I said no.

It wasn't loud or dramatic. Just a firm, steady no. But it was a turning point. Because for the first time in my life, I wasn't swallowing my truth to make other people comfortable.

Looking back now, that was the start of self-leadership. The first time I drew a circle around myself and said, This is where I stand.

That single no would change the course of everything that came next.

BEFORE THE STORM

I was born Joanne Toakley, the youngest of three kids in a house where my dad's presence – and absence – shaped everything.

Dad was an engineer, driven and rarely home. He left early, came back late. We were lucky if we saw him before bed or at the dinner table. His absence was loud. When he was home, he was controlling. My mother had no voice. I didn't realise that until years later, after he died.

He clashed with my oldest brother because they were so alike. He didn't understand my next brother because he was so different. And me? I sat quietly, watching it all. Silent conflict. Loud conflict. Not huge arguments, but enough for me to learn early that it was safer to shrink than to speak.

That was my normal.

Dad didn't ask for opinions. He gave instructions. In 1974, he came home and told my mother: 'I've sold the house, the dogs are sold, we're moving.'

No conversation. No collaboration. No right of reply. Just a statement. And so, we moved.

I was smart at school, no dramas there, but painfully shy. My parents and brothers were loud, and I often felt like I couldn't compete with their energy. I'd retreat to the cupboard because it felt easier to disappear than to try to be heard.

I wanted to go to university, but Dad said no – I had to get a job. So, I sat the bank exams, passed and thought that was it. But Dad had one more lesson in store. He said: 'Now you'll ring every branch manager until you get a job.'

At the time, I thought it was just Dad being Dad – pushy, relentless. What I didn't realise until years later was that this planted one of the most important life lessons I've ever learnt: persistence. Don't wait to be chosen. Knock until the door opens.

Banking became my world. For over twenty years, I worked in commercial banking. It was structured, rule-driven and safe. And yes, I followed the rules. But I also learnt how to back myself. I didn't just sit around waiting to be noticed – when I wanted a promotion or a pay rise, I'd put together a business case for my boss. 'Here's what I've done, here's where I'm going, and this is what I want.' Looking back, that was the start of me learning to use my voice.

At twenty-one, I got married. And here's the truth: I married a man who was a lot like my dad. Controlling. Always needing to be in charge. He didn't like the fact that I was getting further ahead in the bank than he was. He was emotional, volatile and what I now understand as deeply traumatised from his own difficult childhood.

At the time, I just thought I had to manage it, stay quiet, and keep the peace. I just thought it was normal because I didn't know anything different. So I stayed quiet, to keep the peace.

Towards the end of my banking career, I was teaching bankers how to do commercial lending – something almost unheard of for a woman at the time. More than once I was met with the dismissive, 'What do you know, girly?' And yet, I kept showing up, kept teaching, kept holding my ground.

On the outside, I looked strong, capable and successful. On the inside, I was still swallowing my voice.

And that silence would cost me more than I could ever imagine.

THE JOURNEY

After everything fell apart, I didn't expect to find love again. But within twelve months, I met my soulmate.

It wasn't fireworks or fairytales. It was steady. It was kind. It was the first time I felt completely seen. He didn't try to fix me or control me – he stood beside me. That simple shift gave me the courage to stand taller and to try again.

With him, I found the confidence to start taking bigger risks. We opened small ventures first – scrappy, bootstrap attempts that sometimes barely broke even. But each one taught me something: how to sell, how to manage or how to adapt.

We learnt to build on a shoestring, to make mistakes, to pick ourselves up and go again. It wasn't glamorous – but it gave me the resilience muscle I'd later need when the stakes got higher.

Those experiments eventually led to Entamio. And while the headlines called it an 'overnight success', it was really years of grinding, risking and learning in disguise.

It started with an idea, some guts and a vision. Within twenty-four months, it looked like an 'overnight success' – $30 million in turnover. Everyone saw the numbers and assumed I was unstoppable.

But here's the truth: behind the numbers was chaos. I had the clients, the systems, the partners – and yet I was still carrying too much myself. I was white-knuckling decisions, plugging holes and ignoring the toll it was taking on me.

And then the storm hit. A perfect mix of circumstances outside my control collided with cracks on the inside. I was forced to liquidate.

It wiped me clean. Financially. Emotionally. Personally.

People love the 'overnight success' story. Nobody likes to talk about the overnight collapse. But that was my reality.

The day of the liquidation is etched in me.

No Zoom or Teams back then – just me standing in front of my Brisbane office with a commander phone on speaker, the other fifty or sixty staff dialled in from offices down the eastern seaboard.

I told them the truth: we had to liquidate. My hand was forced. The doors were closing that day.

And then something came out of my mouth that I hadn't planned. Maybe it was desperation, maybe instinct. I said, 'If we could just sell off the furniture before the liquidators step in, I could at least pay some of you a bit more salary. Who would be willing to stay back for the next week to help?'

In the room, they all said yes. On the phone, more than 90% of the staff said yes.

And then they did something I'll never forget. The people in Brisbane formed a tight circle around me. They hugged me, crying. They weren't angry. They weren't even asking about their jobs – which they'd just lost a month before Christmas. They were sad for me.

I went upstairs to my office, sat in a chair – half-crying, half-curled up – and felt like I had failed everyone. Then someone from my senior team walked in and handed me a card.

He said, 'We bought this yesterday, before we even knew about today. We could see you were struggling. We just wanted you to know: we love you, we support you, we're here for you.'

That was the slap across the back of the head. The epiphany. The moment I realised: I did something right here. I had built an extraordinary team who supported me, who cared for me, who chose to stand with me – even in the collapse.

And that was the lesson. Your team is always watching. How you show up matters more than the numbers, the wins and the so-called 'success'. What you model is what people carry.

In that moment, I understood something I'd missed for years: leadership isn't just about the growth curve. It's about the circle you build around you and whether they choose to stay when everything falls apart.

THE TRANSFORMATION

Liquidation didn't destroy me. It revealed me.

It stripped away the illusion that success is about revenue, headcount or prestige. It forced me to see that the same patterns that silenced me at my husband's funeral – don't speak up, don't rock the boat, carry it all yourself – had followed me into business.

For years, I thought business was linear. You start, you build, you scale. Straight lines, upward graphs. That's what I'd been taught in banking. That's what I thought success looked like.

But life isn't linear. Business isn't either. It's circular.

If you don't change how you lead yourself, you just keep repeating the same patterns – only with bigger numbers and higher stakes.

And here's the thing: women are often taught to hide failure. To carry shame quietly. To only show the wins, never the wounds. That silence is dangerous. Isolation is dangerous.

In the days after liquidation, the silence was deafening. One day I was the leader of a $30 million company, the next day I was just Joanne – a woman staring at empty offices, who had creditors calling and the sound of my own shame echoing louder than anything.

For a while, I hid. I thought maybe I wasn't cut out for business. I thought maybe I'd proven my critics right. But little by little, I realised:

the liquidation hadn't erased my ability, it had revealed where I'd been building without support.

Looking back, every step of growth in my life came when I wasn't alone. When there was someone beside me who could see what I couldn't. Someone who helped me catch the blind spots. Someone who reminded me of my own voice when I'd gone quiet.

That's the truth I finally had to face: I didn't need more hustle. I needed a circle.

So I started to rebuild my work with a different blueprint. Instead of trying to be the lone hero, I leaned into community, mentorship, and collaboration.

That's how *Her Transformation* was born.

I didn't want to create another 'program'. I wanted to create what I wish I'd had when I left corporate, built my first business, and fell flat on my face trying to do it all alone. I wanted women to have a circle. A place where they could be seen, stretched, supported – and never silenced.

This time, I knew I couldn't do it alone. I deliberately brought in five mentors whose wisdom matched the exact pieces I had been missing:

Energy and intuition – because burnout hides the answers.

Visibility and personal brand – because how you show up matters as much as what you know.

Speaking your story with power.

Unravelling unconscious bias and inherited narratives.

Strategy aligned to your natural strengths.

Together, they form a circle of transformation. Real women with lived wisdom, not just theory.

That's why the circle is deliberate. It's built from the blind spots I once ignored – so that no woman has to walk into them alone.

Circle is no longer just a metaphor for me. It's the method. The thing that changes everything.

Because the truth is, we were never meant to build alone.

THE BACKYARD PEACE PROJECT: VOL 1

FROM MY CIRCLE TO YOURS

If there's one thing my story has taught me, it's this: you can lose everything and still rise again.

I've been the woman silenced at a funeral.

I've been the woman who built a $30 million company and then liquidated it.

I've been the woman curled up in a chair, crying, convinced I had failed.

And I've also been the woman who discovered that even in collapse, I had built something that mattered: a circle of people who stood beside me.

That's the power of circle.

It's not new. Women have gathered in circles for centuries – to share stories, to heal, to pass on wisdom. Somewhere along the way, we forgot. We started building in isolation, believing we had to do it all ourselves. And that isolation has been breaking us.

The modern version of those ancient circles is what I now hold space for. A place where women grow businesses differently. Together.

To the woman reading this who left corporate because you'd had enough, who started your own business determined to do it better, and who now finds herself exhausted: you are not broken. You're just building alone.

You don't need to.

That's why I created Her Transformation. It's not a course. It's not another 'program'. It's a circle – with me and five mentors who bring the exact wisdom I wish I'd had. It's a space where women grow differently. Together.

You don't need to wait until collapse teaches you the hard way.

You don't need to figure it out in silence.

You were never meant to do this alone.

You were meant to rise in circle.

And the circle is waiting.

ABOUT JOANNE

From silence to circle.

In From Silence to Circle, Joanne Brooks shares her raw and unfiltered journey from silence to self-leadership.

As the youngest child in a household ruled by her father's control and absence, Joanne learned early that it was safer to stay quiet than to speak. That pattern followed her into adulthood – through a controlling marriage, the devastating loss of her husband, and the shattering revelation of secrets that left her silenced at his funeral.

But silence could not hold forever. A single, steady no at thirty-eight marked the turning point in Joanne's life. From there, she rebuilt – finding love, launching multiple businesses and ultimately scaling one company to $30 million in just two years before watching it collapse in liquidation.

That collapse became her greatest teacher. It revealed that success without support is fragile and that true leadership isn't linear – it's circular.

Today, Joanne is the founder of Her Transformation, a mentoring circle designed for women who have left corporate life to build businesses differently. With honesty, grit and hard-won wisdom, Joanne's story is a testament to resilience – and to the power of circles in helping women rise.

THE BACKYARD PEACE PROJECT: VOL 1

Joanne Brooks is an entrepreneur, mentor and circle builder with a career shaped by both extraordinary success and profound setbacks. After more than two decades in commercial banking, she went on to launch seventeen businesses – one of which she scaled to $30 million in just two years before facing the harsh reality of liquidation. That experience became her greatest teacher, revealing the importance of resilience, clarity and community.

Today, Joanne is the founder of Her Transformation, a mentoring program designed for women who have left corporate life to build businesses on their own terms. She believes business isn't linear – it's circular – and that women grow stronger when they grow together. With her no-BS approach and lived experience, Joanne empowers female entrepreneurs to find their voice, build with intention and rise in circle, not in isolation.

navig8biz.com

JENNIFER SHARP

BELONGING

This was a topic of conversation today, and boy, did it open a can of worms for me.

Do I belong? Somewhere? Anywhere?

Who am I as a human being?

Who am I in my family?

Am I the odd one out?

If so, why am I?

Why is it that I have always preferred being friends with creatures that have fur, four legs, and a tail?

So many questions swirled inside of me.

When I was asked about what 'belonging' means to me, I was initially at a loss, finding this subject difficult to speak about. But then my mind wandered back to being a little girl who held out each day of the week for Sunday to come so our weekly visit to grandma and grandad would happen.

And then I smiled. This is where I belong.

Inside their house. Smelling grandma's cooking and sitting on grandad's knee at the end of the old dining table, his arms around me, reading and telling stories together.

He listened. I shared.

He shared. I listened.

He always told me that with knowledge came wisdom, and this wisdom could always be found in story.

Grandad was my emotional safety net. He always understood me. His voice, always lyrical, as he read and told stories to me in as many ways as he could.

Cherished moments that ended too soon.

One day, I was told we couldn't go to grandma and grandad's house anymore. I was stunned. Did I do something wrong? Why did they not want to see me? Why did grandad not want to share stories anymore?

Then, grandad never came home from wherever he was. He was just gone.

I didn't know at the time that he had died in the hospital. A heart attack.

On the day of the funeral, I remember being told I had to go to the neighbour's until mum and dad arrived back home. They told me they were going to see grandad one last time. This didn't make any sense to me. Where had he gone? Why did he not tell me he was going anywhere? WHY COULD I NOT SEE HIM?

I recall yelling these words but not getting any response. The neighbour came and literally dragged me to her house – I was extremely distraught at this time, constantly being told to be quiet, this was something that adults did, and to stop being insolent. I remember growing angrier and angrier – I was boiling over until the neighbour yelled over the top of me – HE'S DEAD.

I froze.

I understood the finality of these words. What I couldn't understand is why they didn't tell me.

Mum and dad arrived home with stony faces. I didn't dare ask any questions. I feared what response I would get, or if I would get a response at all. The hours and days that followed came and went like nothing had happened. His name was never mentioned again, and the few times I tried to talk about grandad, I was cut down.

I was only eight when grandad passed.

Sundays lost their existence.

The family dynamics forever changed.

Throughout primary school, as much as I tried, being extra good or extra naughty, doing whatever it took for attention, it never arrived. I was well fed and clothed, had everything material I could ever want. But that's where it stopped. The last hug I got was from grandad. I don't know what a hug is from my parents. I lost trust in relationships, and throughout the years, I often role-played 'families' along with my dolls and teddies, and the very patient cat. I would look after them, read to them, give them sustenance and an extra cuddle, especially at night. I'd pick up on what the other kids at school were saying about their families and pretend mine was the same. I learned not to speak, not to share any emotions – good, negative or indifferent. I was just there at the dinner table for meals and cleaning up, present but not present. I was the youngest in the family, and a girl – my life didn't matter.

One day, coming home from school in the final year of primary, I was so proud of myself. I had been sent to the principal to show him a poem I had written. He gave me three stars (the maximum) and wrote lovely words about it. This was a BIG DEAL. It was a rare occurrence for him to do this, so it was a special honour.

Beaming with pride, I showed mum. I really wanted her to approve of it. Of me. Of something I had done. It was winter. She threw it in the fire, spitting out words something like, 'I don't want to see that rubbish.'

Why did I always feel the need to prove myself? I thought love was meant to be unconditional. Why wasn't she interested in me? Why couldn't I talk to her? What did I do for her to hate me? Why did she bother having me?

I slipped more into reclusiveness and went through high school with the librarian being my best friend. In many but different ways, she rekindled my love of story and sense of belonging. I would often get myself into trouble the day before sports day, as the consequence was to sit in the library, in solitary confinement. Of course, I was in my element! I would sit and write stories, then after a while I would staple the pages together as a book and shelve them. The librarian eventually picked up on what I was doing, and when I went to check out books she'd say to me, 'You might want to pay particular attention to that one,' as she pointed to a book and smiled. Inside would be my story. She was giving me feedback! It was our little game. To this day, I don't know her name, but I am so grateful to have known her.

That was the upside of high school. I was always good at english and art, often getting my poems into the school magazine, but not so much at mathematics. Unfortunately for me, my year ten and year eleven advisor was also the career counsellor, and male. The high school girl's counsellor, I was made to speak with once – because I didn't socialise with the other girls, expressing quite openly that I didn't want to become 'like them' — preferring the characters in my books and stories to be my friends, didn't go down so well. Mum was called up to the school. With a thunderous face, she walked in, listened to the principal and counsellor, and then we left. There was no conversation, no – 'what's going on? Are you okay?' Just anger and silence.

Next, I was to see the career counsellor about work experience. This counsellor was also my maths teacher. When asked what I wanted to do for work experience, I indicated I'd like to spend two weeks with a kindergarten teacher. He laughed, stating I shouldn't be wasting anyone's time, indicating that I would come to be no more than a 'checkout chick' – no disrespect at all to those who do that work! But he eventually did approve of me going into a kindergarten class. I told him I'd already spoken to a school close to my home (lied through my teeth), so we filled out the paperwork. All was well until Mum found out that I had lied about it. Once again, I got a lecture from her and 'what would the neighbours think!'

I simply didn't respond. I had learned from the time grandad died not to show any emotion at all. To anything. Not in facial expression, body language, or with words. Silence for me had become golden. It was my friend.

Being told by teachers that an academic life was for the boys, I dropped out of school halfway through year eleven. I didn't tell my parents for a few days. I knew what the consequences would be. I then went and worked as that 'checkout chick' for three years. I didn't fare too well at this, though – I knew I was destined for more. My mind kept wandering back to grandad and our days together, and something kept stirring within me.

I had been attending a bridging class at university on my day off that gave me the qualification to get into a bachelor's degree where I studied a bachelor of arts majoring in linguistics and education then completing another year after that doing honours in linguistics and a diploma of education that allowed me to teach primary school with an emphasis on early childhood.

I knew it was my soul purpose at that time to work with young children, to show them the love and care, and the power of story, and the feeling of belonging, being in a safe place, and being understood and listened to as I had learned with grandad.

I also remember I broke down and cried when I graduated. I didn't attend my graduation. Even though when I received my piece of paper in the post, and gave the finger to Mr D, the math teacher, along with a few choice words, I didn't feel worthy of it. I was the child, now adult, who chose not to speak, not to communicate with my peers unless I had to, who chose not to show or feel any emotion. Who was I to teach little people?

Grandad. He gave me a voice. He allowed me to be seen and heard and to feel loved, and that I belonged in this world. I was his 'Little Booksy' that's what he always called me. And books and the power of sharing stories are what I was going to do with my life.

THE BACKYARD PEACE PROJECT: VOL 1

After several years of teaching and gaining a research master's degree in special education, I watched my children graduate from school and go on their way. Then tragedy struck. The Toowoomba/Lockyer Valley 2011 floods. I lost my house, my classroom of several years. All my books. I'd lost grandad again.

On compassionate grounds, I was transferred to another school on the coast, where I still live today. During this time, dad became unwell. I took some time off work to support him and, ultimately, mum. I eventually resigned and turned to publishing during this time. It was a no-brainer for me to go from teaching to publishing. It was simply a continuation of telling stories.

Whilst looking after my parents, Covid hit the world, and another personal turning point struck me hard. My health was crumbling. I was giving and giving to others but neglecting myself. I have been a chronic migraine sufferer all my life. One night, I went to bed with a full-blown migraine – the aurors, blurry vision, and half my face was numb. I woke early hours of the morning wanting to vomit. Nothing unusual about that. Except it was different. I was disoriented. Getting to the bathroom was hard, everything was upside down and back the front. Migraines had always occurred on the right side of my head; this one was on the left. I remember vomiting violently, then waking up in the hospital. It was 19 December 2020. To this day, I have no recollection of collapsing on the bathroom floor, of being in an ambulance, or the ER.

After four days of tests, a neurologist came and sat on my hospital bed and showed me an MRI scan of my brain. He pointed to two places on the screen – 'You've had not one, but two strokes.' He pointed to a small lesion in the balance area. Then he pointed to another, bigger lesion – in the language area. I was devastated. But how was this possible? I was talking, thinking, texting. I was a teacher. A publisher. A linguist. I work with words! SHIT.

I was diagnosed with a rare chronic illness that came with three specialists and a dose of four medications every day.

All I could think at the time was I needed to get back to my parents. They were left looking after my cats and dogs. The doctors allowed me to leave on Christmas Eve with many promises of contacting the Stroke foundation and many other places I was referred to.

There was no greeting when I got home from the humans. Life just went on. I just kept going. After all, isn't that what women do? I went back to the same routine of playing the carer and putting myself second. I didn't feel worthy of being cared about.

But deep inside, I knew I was because thoughts of grandad always reminded me I was somebody. I had three degrees, I was a respected teacher, a mum, a grandmother. A year to the day of my health crisis, I remember going to bed, sitting up, and crying like I had never cried before. It had taken me this long to acknowledge what happened and that I wasn't ok. And I missed grandad. I needed him to be with me. Here I was, a grown woman with kids of her own, crying for her grandad, and all he represented, the unconditional love, the belonging. The hugs. I needed to feel his arms around me. I realised I was grieving him, what we had, our time together. His compassion and empathy, and love of humanity. I was grieving myself, my life, with the acknowledgement of not feeling like a whole person anymore. Just an educated person with a screwed-up brain.

A week after I arrived home from the hospital, I contacted some women I had been working with to publish their stories. It was still Covid times, and the women's empowerment movement was strong and gaining momentum. So, I thought.

After I told them what happened, three of them withdrew their work, then proceeded to rubbish my name all over socials as being incompetent. So much for women supporting women. I had lost all respect for both men and women at that stage. More than that. I had lost myself. Who was I now? Did I ever really know? Will I ever know who I am?

THE BACKYARD PEACE PROJECT: VOL 1

Not long after Dad passed away, Mum went into a nursing home, and I returned interstate to my home. I was scared. No income. Health was still not great but was being managed. No work. No self-belief.

But as I unpacked boxes of books, I could feel Grandad around me. I could see his smile, feel his hug, and hear his voice saying to me, 'You've got this, little booksy.'

And I do. I reopened my publishing company, expanded to another. Every day I sit at my desk with grandad behind me, and pics of my grandkids painted baby feet in front of me. A generational legacy. We are all here together, surrounded by books, love, story, and belonging.

ABOUT JENNIFER

As a visionary leader and creative innovator, I am deeply passionate about inspiring change and making a global impact through the power of storytelling. With decades of experience in education, publishing and leadership, I bring a wealth of knowledge and expertise to every story I help bring to life – each one infused with unwavering commitment, passion and heart.

I founded Daisy Lane Publishing, a multiple-awardwinning children's publishing house, to inspire young readers by producing meaningful stories that spark curiosity and imagination and celebrate diversity. We are driven by a deep commitment to kindness, resilience, peace and the environment. Every book we publish serves as a testament to the power of storytelling, connecting readers with one another and the planet we share. At Daisy Lane, we collaborate with a global network of storytellers and artists to reflect the vibrant tapestry of modern families, their culture and communities.

Through Soul Essence Global, I have built a hub of creativity and innovation, publishing thought-provoking books that challenge hearts and minds, while leaving a lasting global legacy. Our exclusive 60-90 Days to Published service empowers authors to bring their dream books to life with seamless guidance, heart, passion and purpose. Soul Essence also takes the lead in hosting transformative leadership experiences twice yearly in breathtaking locations around the world, where magical transformations happen instantly, creating opportunities for leaders to grow, connect and accelerate to their full potential.

With a BA in education and linguistics, a diploma of education and a master of special education, I combine my academic background with two decades of experience as an early years educator. This allows me to craft stories and initiatives that resonate deeply with both children and adults. My work has been featured in *YMag, Beam, Motivate, Brainz Magazine, G100* and *28COE*.

I've had the privilege of making significant contributions to both the literary and educational communities. I founded the *Kidlit International* podcast and have launched *Inspiring Minds – Learning through Story* magazine for children, *Kindness Kids/Youth* on YouTube and Beyond the Word Book Talk International. I've published eight of my own books and have mentored many aspiring writers through the writing and publishing process. I'm also involved in the prestigious programs Just Write for Kids Pitch It Competition raising funds for the Indigenous Literacy Foundation, and am ambassador for Forevability and the DANZ Awards. Additionally, I have served as a judge for the Australian Book Industry Awards (ABIA) and have earned recognition through literary awards such as the Varuna House and May Gibbs internships, along with being a finalist for the Ausmumpreneur, Beam and Roar awards.

daisylanepublishing.com
soulessenceglobal.com
linkedin.com/in/jennifer-sharp-publishing-consultant
instagram.com/daisylanepublishing
instagram.com/soul_essence_global_

JENNIFER SHARP

youtube.com/@DaisyLanePublishing
youtube.com/@KindnessKidsWW
youtube.com/@BeyondTheWord-BookTalkInt

JUDY MYERS
WHEN DESTINY FINDS YOU

Earth School continues to remind me that there is always another level to reach …

The wild Southern Ocean crashes below, and it appears that mother nature is delivering a metaphor. Some waters run deep, and though the ocean is calm and peaceful one day, that can change in an instant. Life is just a blink of a moment in time, and moments are fleeting and, like mercury, hard to keep hold of. Just when it feels permanent, you're reminded that nothing is there to be owned.

'All I wish for you is happiness, and if that means you have to walk away from me to attain it, then that is what you must do.'

Tears rolled down my face and pooled around my neck, and my heart felt like it was shattering into a million pieces. A grief-soaked thought broke through: how many times can one heart shatter? It shattered when Gary, my brother who never got to grow up, was killed at eighteen; it shattered when my selfless, hard-working dad was diagnosed with Alzheimer's at fifty-two; it shattered when, at forty-nine, my beautiful, sensitive brother David took his own life; and when my mum transitioned after succumbing to non-Hodgkin's lymphoma, my heart shattered, and a piece of me died with her. My heart shattered when my soulmate, my baby boy Gus, grew his angel wings and crossed the rainbow bridge. The grief surfaced through cellular memory, but it also reminded me of everything I had survived.

As I sat upon the rocky outcrop atop the Bluff, recalling my conversation the previous evening with Shyam, I knew that even if he walked away, my love for him would remain. Love never dies, and I will survive.

Born into a loving, but humble, country family, the youngest of six. I was an aunty at the tender age of eight. Nieces and nephews were part of my life growing up; children gravitated to me, and all I wanted was to be a teacher and be surrounded by them. Today I'm a great, great aunt, and given my intention to live to at least one hundred, I'll one day be a great, great, great, great aunt. Or, as I'd much rather be known: a legendary aunt.

It was just a natural assumption that one day I would have a child or children of my own. Following the family tradition, I married young, just before my twentyieth birthday. I married a lovely man five years older; the type of man that your grandmother and mother love.

Moving to the city to attend university began a stirring deep within me, one I couldn't ignore. A stable, secure, predictable life didn't light me up; in fact, it made me feel claustrophobic. There was a big, beautiful world out there, and I wanted to explore as much of it as possible; learn about other cultures, walk among the ancient ruins, trek through the Amazon, ski the slopes in France, commune with the animals in Galápagos, and ride a Vespa around Santorini.

It was with a heavy heart (who wants to hurt someone they love), yet it also brought a sense of lightness and freedom that I left my marriage and set off on the first of many adventures. (Terry went on to remarry and have a daughter.)

'Say yes to opportunity, then work it out later,' was my mantra. In the words of Sir Richard Branson, 'Saying yes is far more fun than saying no!'

Work adventures took me to over forty countries and many during times of great change. In Namibia, still feeling the dark shadow of apartheid, I facilitated workshops for people who had never spoken to a white person before. In Laos, I was there just after it opened to the

THE BACKYARD PEACE PROJECT: VOL 1

West, I brought along a Polaroid camera. I'll never forget the wonder on people's faces as they saw photographs of themselves for the very first time.

I was living an expansive life, but it was full throttle. I was frequently overseas, running workshops, managing a junior sport program at the Institute of Sport in Canberra, coaching Paralympic athletes and running a martial arts and fitness studio. It was exhilarating and exhausting.

Eventually, my body decided that enough was enough. I ignored the lights flashing on my internal dashboard when I experienced amenorrhoea. My body was saying, 'Something's not right, and I don't feel safe enough to reproduce.' The next warning light to commence flashing was the adrenals, and although I could still function at a high level, my battery never actually recharged. Eventually, chronic fatigue quietly stepped from the shadows and took centre stage, no longer content to be ignored. One day, I was going full speed, and the next, I was bedridden.

When I recovered, I decided perhaps it was time to settle and start a family. After all, the biological clock was echoing at a deafening decibel. After twelve months and still no positive pregnancy test, it became clear something wasn't quite right. My partner, Mark, wasn't keen to investigate. His philosophy was, 'If it's meant to be, it will be.'

It never was.

Mark left to live and work in Vietnam, and I decided our ten-year relationship had run its course. We remained friends, and his parents still considered me their daughter. I even gave him away at his wedding in Vietnam some years later. I love to say I couldn't sell him, so I gave him away. He is the father of two teenage children.

There were days when I would quietly sit on the fringes of gatherings and observe friends and family with their children. On those days, a sadness usually buried deep within would surface and remind me that I would never have that experience.

The day my mother transitioned to her next great adventure, I watched my nieces and nephews gather around my grieving siblings, offering comfort and care. And in that moment, I felt a suffocating wave of profound grief for the loss of my mother and my motherhood. I was now a motherless daughter. And I would always be a childless mother. I would never know the feeling of tiny hands in mine or the sound of little feet running to me, calling 'Mum'.

Although my current partner, Rod, was happy to investigate adoption when we met, I felt it wouldn't be fair. He had raised two adult children, and he was keen for freedom; to be adventurous and travel. He had been waiting years to feel that autonomy.

There was always a question lingering in my mind: Why couldn't I have children? When Mark wasn't willing to investigate the cause back in my early thirties, I just got on with life. But that question never fully left me; it lived quietly in the background.

One of my aunties, my mother's sister, had also been unable to have children. During a conversation with one of my brothers about his granddaughter, who had been trying to conceive for years, I gently suggested that maybe there was a hereditary link.

That's when he dropped a bombshell! 'No, you can't have children because Mum took thalidomide when she was pregnant with you. Two other girlfriends did too, and none of you girls could have kids. Didn't you know?'

No. I didn't know.

My poor darling mother never told me or my sister. If it were true, perhaps she felt ashamed that she took the drug. I hold no anger towards my mum; she had five children to contend with and was often required to drive trucks with Dad. She didn't have time to be sick. While my brother's words left me reeling, I still don't know for certain if it was true.

Through my international work, I realised that, directly or indirectly, I was having a meaningful impact on the lives of children and young people, and it became clear: this was exactly what I was meant to be doing. If I'd had my own family, I would have had to give this up or face the heartbreak of being away for weeks at a time. Maybe I didn't miss out on motherhood after all. Maybe I simply expanded it.

In my forties, I was still spending up to six months a year working internationally, so having a pet made no sense at all, and I had not had a pet since I was a child. A clairvoyant had told me several times over the years that a soul was waiting to join me. I would always gently remind her, 'I can't have children.'

Every magazine or TV ad seemed to feature a woman with a little white dog, riding Vespas, getting massages, or out shopping. They were everywhere. One day, without knowing the breed or considering the consequences, I found myself unexpectedly saying to Rod, 'I want a white dog like that, and his name is Gus.' Once a puppy walks across your heart, it's hard to be away from them for long. After a few more years, I realised that being away from home so often no longer fulfilled me the way it once did. I took on a position at Flinders University, one that still included some international travel to satisfy my love of connecting with different cultures and allowed for longer periods at home.

My role involved developing international business opportunities for the faculty of science and engineering. It was a wonderful balance of global engagement and grounded home living. We had significant research collaboration with Indian universities, and at the time, reports of racism against Indian students in Melbourne and Sydney had received widespread coverage in Indian media. This understandably resulted in families and institutions being cautious about sending students or academics to Australia.

I decided it would be a sound, strategic move to take one of our Indian students with me on my next academic delegation. The executive dean agreed, and I put out an expression of interest to our Indian student cohort. I received several delightful and formal applications from interested students, but one stood out. He left a casual message on my answering machine, and something about the message compelled me to choose him.

Shyamsundar (Shyam) was an excellent choice. Easy to travel with, polite, professional and cheeky. During our three-week visit to Southern India, I learnt that he had lost his mother to kidney disease when he was just ten. His father had done everything he could to save her, but sadly, to no avail. After her passing, Shyam was then raised by his granny on a farm. The farmhouse had only one electric light bulb and no running water. Granny would either bring water from a well a few hundred metres away for Shyam to bathe or he would bathe at the well. His native language is Tamil, and he taught himself English at sixteen to attend college.

When we arrived back in Australia, he said to me that travelling with me was like travelling with his mum. I laughed and pretended to be offended that he thought I could be old enough to be his mum; after doing the math, I was!

Shyam was often at our home, and we loved having him around. Years later, he confessed that he could never quite remember whether the Westie's name was Rod or Gus or whether my partner was Gus or Rod.

One day, while having lunch together at the University, he announced that he had met someone, and they were going to be married. He asked me to be his mum at his wedding. What an honour.

The marriage ceremony was held in a Catholic church, out of respect for his bride's faith, and a vibrant, joyful, Indian reception followed. Shyam bought me a stunning 'Anarkali suit', deep red with delicate gold embroidery. As I stepped into that beautiful outfit, I didn't just feel dressed for the occasion; I felt deeply connected to him and his heritage. It was a moment I will never forget.

Tragedy struck when Shyam was diagnosed with the same kidney disease that had taken his mother. His older brother also had the disease. Shyam had to return to India and await a transplant, undergoing dialysis every second day. To keep his student visa status, he had to return to

Australia for twenty-four hours during this time, carefully timed around his dialysis.

Thankfully, after eighteen months, he was blessed to receive a kidney that his body accepted, and he returned to Australia to continue his life and complete his doctorate.

Over the years, we grew closer. When his marriage ended during COVID, he came to live with us and work from home. What once began as 'this is my Indian son' and 'this is my Aussie mum' eventually became simply 'this is my son' and 'this is my mum'.

I am forever grateful to Shyam's mother, father, granny and older brother for the extraordinary child they raised. He is a beautiful, caring, loving and brilliant human. We're not connected by blood; we're connected by love. His mother gave me the gift of her son. And I will forever be humbled by that.

Earlier this year, Shyam and I returned to India together for the first time since our original academic trip. He had been invited to deliver a presentation at a world nephrology conference in Delhi, and he asked if I would accompany him.

It was a beautiful experience, one I will always treasure, spending time with his father, brother, and his brother's family.

On our first night in Chennai, we visited his brother's home. Inside was a beautiful shrine to their mother. Shyam and I stood together in front of her photo, holding hands as tears quietly fell. It was a moment that will remain with me.

Whether you believe in tarot or not, what Shyam shared with me later touched me at a soul level. He had recently received his one and only tarot reading, and the reader asked him gently, 'Did you lose your mum? Do you have a second mum now?' When he said yes to both these questions, she told him: 'Your mother sent her; she sent her to be your mum.'

During our time in Tamil Nadu, I was able to visit the farmhouse where Shyam had lived with his granny, and the stories he had shared with me over the years came vividly to life.

We also travelled together through majestic Rajasthan, and then onwards to Kerala, India's own Garden of Eden, and his dad was able to travel with us.

Recently, Shyam began a new relationship, and when his life expanded to include a partner, I was thrilled and delighted for them both. My wish has always been for his happiness. The bond Shyam and I share is unique, and it may take time for others to appreciate its depth. Naturally, this has brought moments of adjustment, and Shyam, being the caring and loving person he is, has found himself navigating the emotions of others.

I don't know what the outcome will be, but I do know that my heart and door will always remain open to my son and those he loves. Love is not about possession; it is about acceptance, kindness and compassion. If he walks away to preserve peace in his life, I will let him go with love; he will know he is deeply accepted for who he is. If he returns, I will welcome him back with open arms.

Regardless of what happens, I will forever be grateful for the gift of being called Mum. It was more than I ever imagined.

ABOUT JUDY

My passport is full, my heart is fuller; the world has been my classroom and its lessons have shaped everything I teach.

I'm Judy Myers – coach, traveller, lifelong learner and someone who has built a life on saying yes to the road less travelled. I grew up in country Australia with a restless curiosity that's carried me to more than seventy-five countries, working in over forty of them. From the turquoise lagoons of the Cook Islands to the bustling streets of India, the deserts of Namibia to the high-rises of Doha, I've led leadership workshops, worked alongside communities in times of great change and shared conversations that left a lasting mark on my heart. Each journey has shaped how I see the world and how I help others see themselves.

Freedom to live a life of adventure was, perhaps, the trade-off for not being gifted with the biology to have a child. While that was once a painful chapter, it opened space for a different kind of life; one rich with purpose, travel and connection. And in time, motherhood found me in the most unexpected way.

Coaching has always been in my bones; listening deeply, asking the questions that matter and guiding people to find their own answers. Today, I work with professionals to clear mental clutter, sharpen communication and master their energy so they can lead with presence, purpose and the kind of composure that inspires trust.

None of us are broken. We just get buried under noise, expectation and old patterns. Strip those away, and you uncover the space, energy and courage to create a life that fits, like it was made for you.

Email: judy@judymyerscoaching.com.au
Web: judymyerscoaching.com.au
Facebook: facebook.com/judy.myers2016
LinkedIn: linkedin.com/in/judy-myers-coach

DR JULIE DUCHARME

RISING AUTHENTICALLY
A JOURNEY OF STRUGGLE, RESILIENCE AND EMPOWERMENT

A pivotal moment that shaped my perspective on struggle and resilience wasn't just one event – it was the legacy I witnessed through the men in my family. My father and both of my grandfathers were entrepreneurs, but their paths were far from easy.

Both of my grandfathers never made it past the sixth grade. The Great Depression forced them into the workforce at a young age. Grandpa Herb was an immigrant who had a severe stutter, which made it incredibly difficult to be understood – especially while trying to build a life and a business in a new country. My other grandfather, Grandpa Willie, married my grandmother when she was only sixteen, then was shipped off to war for three years, leaving her to navigate life on her own.

Despite their lack of education or formal training, their resilience was powerful. Grandpa Willie later developed a severe form of arthritis that nearly crippled him. But instead of giving up, he adapted – he got himself an electric cart, modified a van so he could still drive and found ways to stay mobile even when his body was nearly frozen in place.

One memory I'll never forget: It was my birthday, and despite all his physical limitations, Grandpa Willie got on his cart, drove it at least a couple of miles and bought me a beautiful music box. I still have it to this day at the age of forty-eight. That act – small to some, but monumental to me – was a lesson in love, determination and the kind of strength that can't be taught in school.

My father, too, is one of the most talented and kindest men I've ever known. After working for large companies, he eventually started his own successful business. What connected all three of these men wasn't just their work ethic – it was how they led with heart. They cared deeply for people, brought joy to their work, and consistently made a difference in their communities.

Watching my grandfathers and father push past every excuse not to move forward – and do so with joy – taught me what kind of person and leader I wanted to be. Their legacy gave me the blueprint for not only building a business, but building a life rooted in resilience, integrity, and impact.

Probably one of the most profound and personal challenges I've ever faced was the loss of my mother. She wasn't just my mom – she was my champion, my biggest fan and, truly, my hero.

Despite being disabled by a painful disease, she never let it define her. Like my grandfather, she got herself a cart and found a way to serve others – especially the people no one else wanted to serve. She would drive her cart into the toughest parts of town, delivering care packages to the homeless. She organised fundraisers to help girls who couldn't afford prom to buy dresses and cover their tickets. She knit hats for cancer patients. And she had a prayer line – if someone was in need, she'd rally everyone she knew to pray for them.

My mom never used her pain or disability as an excuse. She served because it was who she was – deeply compassionate, humble and driven by love. When she passed away unexpectedly twelve years ago, I was devastated. My world turned upside down. I had two little children who would never get to know her or feel the depth of her love for them. I couldn't call her anymore to ask if my kids were doing things 'right' or send her pictures so she could cheer them on. It was a grief like no other.

But in the midst of that pain, I realised something: the best way

I could honour my mom was to carry the torch she left behind. The torch of service. The torch of compassion. The torch of bringing people together.

So twelve years ago, I started taking small steps towards becoming a servant leader. I didn't know it at the time, but that moment of loss was planting the seed for what would eventually become Lead and Empower Her She Talks – a global organisation serving women around the world. It was through embracing that call to serve – through deciding to lead with love and action – that I began to heal. And in doing so, I found a way to keep my mom with me in everything I do.

Serving others has become the greatest job I've ever had. Because when we serve, we are blessed tenfold. And the legacy we leave – the love, the kindness, the impact – is what truly lasts.

Transitioning from academia to entrepreneurship was one of the most daunting experiences of my life. The cultural shift alone was massive. I had come from a high-powered position where I was constantly needed – my days were packed, my weeks were long, and I was running a multimillion-dollar program. I thrived in the chaos because I was good at bringing order to it. And even though I knew deep down I didn't want to do that work for the next twenty years, I was incredibly good at it.

So when I stepped away from that leadership role and found myself working alone from home, the silence was deafening. I battled anxiety, depression and what I call the epidemic of loneliness. Even with plenty on my to-do list, my days felt strangely empty. I missed being wanted, being needed. I missed the adrenaline of the hustle and the impact I was making every day.

But what finally motivated the shift wasn't just a feeling – it was my health. I was working eighty hours a week while raising a two-year-old and a newborn. My body started breaking down. I developed dangerously high blood pressure, my hair was falling out and my doctor told me bluntly, 'You're on the verge of a heart attack.' Then he asked me something that shook me: 'Do you want to be here to see your kids grow up?'

Of course I did. I had already experienced the deep pain of losing my mother too soon – I couldn't bear the thought of my kids living without me. My doctor looked at me and said, '"hen you need to rethink what success means. Is this kind of success worth it if it costs you your health, your time with your family, your life?;

That moment stopped me in my tracks. He was right. My family meant everything. I knew I had to find a way to have both – a meaningful career and a life I could truly live and enjoy with my family. That's when I reached out to friends and mentors. To my surprise, many of them offered me part-time work to help cover my bills while I figured out how to launch my business. One of those mentors, Dr Freda, was especially pivotal. She believed in me, supported me and guided me through that transition. I'll always be grateful for her encouragement – it helped me step into entrepreneurship and financial freedom without sacrificing my family or losing myself in the process.

As the founder of multiple ventures – including JD Consulting and Synergy Learning Institute – one of the biggest initial struggles I faced was realising that even with an MBA, I wasn't fully prepared for the realities of building a business from the ground up. My degree taught me how to run large organisations, but those roles had infrastructure already in place – I was simply plugging into an existing system. Starting my own company was a completely different experience.

When I launched my first business over twenty-three years ago, the landscape was vastly different. The internet was just emerging, and we didn't have the powerful digital tools and platforms we rely on today. Everything was manual – research, outreach, marketing and operations. I had to rely heavily on instinct, trial and error, and a lot of long nights doing things the hard way.

To make it even more challenging, the types of businesses I was building were relatively new in the market. There wasn't a clear road map – I was often creating one as I went. But I've always believed I was meant to be an entrepreneur. I call it my 'sixth sense' for business. I have a natural ability to see gaps, identify opportunities and build innovative solutions.

With each company I started, I was solving a real-world problem. The initial challenge was always, 'How do I solve this in a way that's scalable and impactful?' I didn't want to create something so niche that only a small group could benefit. I wanted to solve problems that made life better for a broad audience.

What helped me push through those early hurdles was a combination of grit, creativity and support. I was fortunate to have mentors and friends who believed in me, but I also leaned heavily on my own zone of genius – thinking outside the box. That creative thinking allowed me to scale my businesses in unique ways, offer innovative programs and bring bold visions to life.

Those early struggles weren't easy – but they sharpened my instincts, deepened my resilience and reminded me that true success comes from solving real problems with heart, strategy, and vision.

As an entrepreneur, I could give you a long list – challenges are simply part of the journey when you're building and growing a business. One of the most difficult moments for me was the impact of COVID, which hit several of my companies hard. It forced me to rethink my approach, pivot and rebuild from devastation. But another moment that truly tested my inner strength came from trusting the wrong person. I met a very vibrant woman who seemed passionate about doing good and pitched an idea for a program. I believed in her vision, and since I was great at building programs, I agreed to help her. It seemed like a win-win. I built the entire program for very little money, trusting that once it launched, we'd make up the difference on the back end.

But as time went on, I realised her superpower was convincing others to do the work – without ever paying them. The more I saw how things were unfolding, the more I recognised I needed to step away. I was exhausted, unpaid, and the program – while growing – was ultimately hers to run. I decided to exit gracefully, allowing her to take over the reins.

Unfortunately, instead of a peaceful hand-off, she turned on me. She told members I had stolen money, encouraged them to claim fraud with their banks, and as a result, I lost over $20,000. I provided evidence and fought every claim, but the banks sided with the customers, leaving me in debt and emotionally devastated.

I remember sitting on my back porch in tears, questioning everything. I had believed in her. I thought she stood for the same values I did. For someone to slander me and twist the truth after I had poured everything into helping her – it shook me deeply. My moral and ethical compass is everything to me. I operate from a place of servant leadership. I often give more than I receive because I believe in making a difference, but being painted as a thief was almost more than I could bear.

I was ready to walk away from it all.

Thankfully, I reached out to a trusted friend and business mentor. I remember his words clearly: 'You need to let it go. It's not worth going to small claims court. Look at how this is tearing you up. You've helped thousands of women – don't let one person undo all of that. The people who know you, who know your heart; that has to be enough. Move forward.'

He was right. It wasn't easy, but I chose to release the anger, the grief and the betrayal. I reminded myself why I started in the first place. Yes, my willingness to believe in people has burned me at times, but more often than not, it has created powerful, lasting impact. I've helped transform lives – and those people have changed mine in return.

I wouldn't trade this journey of entrepreneurship for anything. It's been hard, yes – but also the most rewarding experience of my life. And I hope to leave behind a legacy of strength, authenticity and service for all those who come after me.

Honestly, I think the She Talks movement was growing inside of me long before I ever realised it. Even as a little girl, I was curious, independent and full of big dreams. My parents never put limits on me – they encouraged me to imagine a future without boundaries. And if you could've seen inside my young entrepreneur brain back then, it would've been overwhelming. I had huge visions, even as a small-town farm girl. From an early age, I naturally stepped into leadership roles. But in many spaces – especially male-dominated ones – I was often shut down. Even more painfully, I faced resistance from other young women. Looking back now, I realise that much of it came from their own insecurity, but at the time, it was deeply hurtful. I was often sabotaged by the very people I thought I was aligned with. Thankfully, I was stubborn and driven. Settling for average was never an option for me.

As I grew older, I continued entering male-dominated industries and environments – not to prove something, but because that's where my dreams led me. I didn't care how hard it was. I was ready for the battle. It's just who I am.

By the time I reached what many would call the pinnacle – leading in the corporate world by the age of thirty – I had a realisation that stopped me in my tracks: women were still terrible to each other. I had experienced it all the way up the ladder. And while I don't think I was ever intentionally unkind, I'm sure I contributed to the competitive energy that left no room for collaboration.

Then I had my daughter.

Something shifted in me. I suddenly saw the world through her eyes and asked myself: 'Do I want her to go through what I did?' The answer was no. I wanted her to grow up in a world where women supported each other, collaborated, celebrated one another and built together.

That led me to ask the hardest question of all: 'What have I done to contribute to that kind of world for women?'

And I didn't have an answer. That realisation shook me.

I knew we had to change the paradigm. I was told repeatedly, 'Julie, you can't change this culture.' But I had to try. I still have to try.

The journey hasn't been easy. There have been tears, heartbreak and moments of deep frustration – especially when other women tried to tear down what I was building. But my daughter remains my driving force. She reminds me that the fight is worth it.

I believe that as women, we are capable of so much more. We can build better together. Our loyalty – when we choose to show up for each other – is unmatched. And that's what She Talks is all about: rewriting the narrative of competition into one of collaboration, empowerment and lasting legacy.

That's such a great question – how do you define empowerment?

If you Google it, the definition says: 'The process of becoming stronger and more confident, especially in controlling one's life and claiming one's rights.' And while I agree with that, I've learnt over the years that empowerment is deeply personal and can look different for everyone. What empowers me might not empower someone else – and that's okay. What really struck me, especially as we went global with She Talks, is that when you strip away religion, culture and politics, at our core we as women are the same. I know that may sound hard to believe, but across borders and backgrounds, I've seen it firsthand – we all share similar aspirations. We want to succeed in our careers, be great mothers, partners, leaders and human beings. We dream, we strive, we love deeply. In essence, we all want to live with purpose and fulfilment.

And that is empowerment – recognising that shared humanity.

So I don't feel like I have to 'employ' empowerment as a strategy. I live it. I speak my truth, I show up with passion, and I create space for other women to do the same. That in itself is empowering. When women see someone being raw, real and unapologetically authentic, it gives them permission to do the same.

One of the most powerful tools I use is storytelling. I believe the most impactful way we empower others is by sharing our true, authentic stories – not the polished version, but the real one. I've watched women come alive just by hearing that they're not alone in their struggles, dreams or doubts.

Ultimately, empowerment isn't about giving someone power – it's about reminding them that they already have it. My role is simply to reflect that back to them.

Before you can truly embrace your authentic self, you first have to know who that is. And that's not always easy. I've found that as we grow – through our twenties, thirties and beyond – our experiences shape and reshape us. What I wanted at twenty looked completely different by twenty-three, and by thirty, I had evolved again.

I've had a lot of transitions in my life – each one tied to those experiences. But truthfully, I don't think I fully embraced my true authentic self until I was close to forty. And let me tell you, that realisation was terrifying. What would people think? Would they still support me? Like me? Follow me?

But that's where the journey had to start – with letting go of what others thought.

I had to stop living for others' expectations and start showing up as who I really was. That meant shifting my focus, rebranding myself and getting honest about what I wanted. And yes, imposter syndrome came knocking – loudly. But I knew something was missing in my life. I kept saying to myself, 'There has to be something more.'

Once I embraced that decision, a tremendous sense of freedom followed. The weight of trying to meet everyone else's expectations lifted. I stopped moulding myself into what others needed me to be and started becoming the woman I was meant to be – the one others were naturally drawn to because I was real, grounded and aligned.

That shift transformed everything. My mindset changed. My joy increased. My business more than doubled – because people weren't just buying into a brand, they were connecting with me. My authenticity created a space where others wanted to belong and grow.

And maybe the biggest gift? For the first time, I felt like I was truly living. Not just existing. Not just performing. But living fully and freely.

That transformation didn't just impact me – it became the catalyst for helping others do the same. By stepping into my authentic self, I gave others permission to do the same. And that ripple effect has been the most rewarding part of all.

Today, I wake up every morning without regret. I know that whenever my time here ends, I will have lived this life to the fullest – as the best version of myself.

I remember the very first time I truly stepped into my authentic self – it was when I wrote my first non-academic book. That moment was a turning point for me. I made the decision to stop hiding behind perfection and start telling the truth: about my body image issues, my insecurities, and the pressure I felt to be everything to everyone.

What pushed me to write it was the unexpected loss of a friend—someone we all believed had the 'perfect' life. Her death by suicide shook us to the core. I remember thinking, *If she was struggling and none of us knew, what about me?*

The truth was, I was struggling too. I was silently breaking under the pressure. I cried in the shower so no one would hear. I strived for the perfect house, perfect children, and to be the perfect wife and mom – because that's what I thought was expected of me. From the outside, it looked like I had it all together. But inside, I was unravelling.

Writing that book gave me permission to stop pretending. It allowed me to not only share my struggles but also share how I began to make real changes. It became a road map – not just for me, but for other women – to start their own journey towards authenticity.

And the transformation didn't stop at the page.

I changed how I dressed, choosing clothes that made me feel confident. I changed who I worked with and how I worked. I aligned my life and my business with what felt true to who I really was – not who others expected me to be.

For me, it was a big, bold transformation. But I've learnt that for many women, it can start with something small – a shift in how they speak to themselves, how they show up, or how they set boundaries. Those small shifts build momentum and eventually lead to a life of alignment and truth.

To maintain my authenticity, I practise constant self-check-ins. I ask: 'Does this align with my values? Am I doing this out of obligation or from a place of truth?' I've also surrounded myself with people who celebrate the real me, not the curated version. Authenticity, for me, is now non-negotiable. And the positive outcome? I've built a life – and a legacy – that is deeply rooted in truth, connection and freedom. And I've helped other women do the same.

One of the core ways I maintain authenticity is by making sure everything I do aligns with who I truly am and the journey I'm on. I only say yes to opportunities, projects and partnerships that reflect my values and vision. If something doesn't feel aligned with my authentic self, I have no problem walking away – no matter how popular or profitable it may seem.

I also surround myself with people who fit into that same authentic space – those who support, uplift and challenge me in the right ways. I'm very protective of my energy and the company I keep because it directly impacts how I show up in the world.

Another non-negotiable for me is my ethics and personal standards. I stick to them, even when it's uncomfortable or when saying no might not be the popular response. I'm not here to please everyone – I'm here to be me, to stand in truth and to help others step into the life they were meant to live.

So for me, maintaining authenticity isn't complicated. It's actually pretty simple: If it aligns, I say yes. If it doesn't, I don't. I trust myself, I trust my values, and I stay rooted in them.

I consider myself a democratic and servant leader, and I believe the combination of these two styles is what allows me to lead effectively—especially during uncertain times.

If we unpack these leadership styles, here's what you'll find:

- Democratic leadership is centred around shared decision-making. It values open communication, diverse perspectives and collaboration. It fosters a sense of ownership and empowerment among team members, which leads to higher engagement and morale.
- Servant leadership, on the other hand, is all about prioritising the growth, wellbeing and development of your team. It's about placing their needs above your own and creating a supportive, inclusive environment where people can thrive.

Together, these styles create a leadership approach that's rooted in trust, empowerment and collaboration – exactly what's needed during times of uncertainty.

As Simon Sinek says, 'Leaders eat last.' That's a principle I live by. I empower my team members to embrace their roles using their unique strengths and genius. I don't micromanage – but I'm always there to offer support, guidance and mentorship when needed. I believe that if your team is successful, you are successful. So I focus on building their confidence, giving them the tools they need and helping them stay grounded in what they do best. When people know they're supported, when they're clear on their value and when they feel empowered to make decisions – they become naturally resilient and adaptable.

Uncertainty will always come. But if you've trained your people to lead with confidence, to lean into their strengths and to trust that they have what it takes, they will rise to the challenge. As a leader, your role isn't to control everything. It's to create the kind of environment where others can thrive no matter what comes their way.

For me, decision-making – whether in business or life – always comes back to a few core, non-negotiable values: authenticity, integrity, service, courage and faith.

- Authenticity is at the centre of everything I do. I refuse to wear masks or fit into moulds that don't reflect who I am. I make choices that align with my purpose, my voice and my vision – even if it's not the most popular path.
- Integrity is everything. I do what I say I will do, and I hold myself accountable. I've walked away from opportunities that didn't feel ethically right, even when it was a sacrifice, because I believe that keeping your character intact is far more valuable than any deal or partnership.
- Service is why I lead. I don't build just to build – I build to empower others. Whether I'm working with a client, mentoring a leader or guiding my team, I ask: 'How can this serve someone else?' That shift in perspective always leads to better outcomes.
- Courage shows up in my willingness to say no, take risks and challenge the status quo. Every big step in my career and personal life required me to do something uncomfortable. I've learnt that if fear shows up, it means I'm on the edge of growth.
- Faith keeps me grounded. I trust that everything unfolds for a reason, even when I can't see the full picture. That spiritual compass helps me stay calm and focused despite the chaos.

These values aren't just words on paper – they're filters I use daily to check my intentions, actions and direction. And when I'm aligned with these values, I know I'm leading in a way that honours who I am and the legacy I want to leave.

For me, peace wasn't something I stumbled upon – it was something I earned through struggle.

Life didn't hand me ease; it handed me challenges, heartbreaks, setbacks and hard lessons. But it was through those exact moments that I found my strength and, ultimately, my peace.

I've been through personal betrayals, professional losses and seasons where everything I built felt like it was crumbling. I've been the woman crying in the shower, holding it all together on the outside while falling apart on the inside. But what I've learnt through every one of those experiences is that struggle refines you. It strips away what doesn't serve you and reveals what truly matters.

Peace came when I stopped trying to be perfect and started being honest. It came when I let go of needing approval and began living in alignment with my values. It came when I stopped asking, 'Why is this happening to me?' and started asking, 'What is this trying to teach me?'

I found peace through faith, through purpose and through service to others. I learnt that I don't have to have all the answers to keep moving forward. I just need to stay grounded in who I am, keep showing up and trust the process – even when it's messy.

Today, peace doesn't mean my life is without problems. It means I've made peace with who I am, how far I've come and the journey I'm still on. I've learnt to see struggle not as a roadblock – but as a teacher. And through every lesson, I've found more of myself.

That's how I found peace – not by avoiding the struggle, but by walking through it with open arms, open heart and unshakable purpose.

Mindfulness and self-reflection are essential tools in how I overcome adversity – they allow me to pause, process and pivot with purpose instead of reacting out of fear or frustration. As a leader, a mom and a business owner, life doesn't stop throwing challenges, but I've learnt that how I show up in the face of those challenges makes all the difference.

Mindfulness grounds me in the present moment. When chaos hits, I take a breath, step back, and ask: 'What's really happening here? What is this trying to teach me?' That moment of stillness often gives me clarity

I wouldn't find in the noise.

Self-reflection is where growth happens. I carve out intentional time to reflect on what worked, what didn't and how I responded – especially during hard times. I journal, I pray and I seek out feedback. And sometimes, I just sit in the discomfort long enough to understand what's underneath it. That self-awareness makes me a stronger, more empathetic leader.

Mindfulness and reflection don't remove adversity – but they help me rise above it with purpose, resilience and grace. They remind me that even in struggle, there's an opportunity to align deeper with who I am and what I'm here to do.

My advice is simple but powerful: Don't let struggle convince you that you're off track – sometimes, the hardest seasons are the most important parts of your purpose journey.

Struggle refines you, clarifies your calling and strips away what doesn't serve you. Peace isn't the absence of struggle; it's the presence of alignment – even when things are hard.

When you're in the middle of it, remind yourself: you're not broken – you're becoming. Stay close to your values, stay grounded in your 'why' and surround yourself with people who speak life into you, not fear. You don't have to have it all figured out to take the next step. Peace comes from owning who you are, standing in your truth and refusing to settle for less than the life you're meant to live.

Keep going – you're closer than you think.

Struggle has never been a stop sign for me – it's been a signal to dig deeper, pivot, and grow.

As I move forward, I plan to keep leaning into transparency and storytelling – sharing not just the wins, but the hard parts too. That's where connection and transformation really happen.

In my work, I'll continue building platforms that turn pain into purpose – whether that's through She Talks, leadership coaching or empowering others to share their stories. Personally, I'll keep doing the inner work: staying grounded, reflecting and aligning my actions with my values.

I believe in creating spaces where people can grow through what they go through. That's the mission – turning adversity into action and using every challenge as a tool for greater impact.

ABOUT DR JULIE

Dr Julie Ducharme is a dynamic leader, keynote speaker, national bestselling author and serial entrepreneur with over twenty years of experience in empowering others to achieve their fullest potential. She is the visionary behind the Lead and Empower Her SHE Talks movement, a nationwide women's empowerment conference that has inspired countless women to find their voice, share their stories and take control of their personal and professional destinies. Dr Ducharme's commitment to uplifting women led her to create SHE Talks, a platform that provides women with opportunities to speak, write and be featured in impactful ways – from contributing chapters to national book series to being spotlighted in *SHE Talks* magazine.

An expert in leadership, Dr Ducharme holds a doctorate in business and has spent her career working with individuals and organisations to redefine leadership and break down barriers. Whether she's leading executive workshops, delivering keynote speeches or mentoring the next generation of female entrepreneurs, her message is clear: women have the power to shape industries, communities and futures when they step into their authentic leadership.

Dr Ducharme's entrepreneurial spirit has also driven her to build multiple successful ventures. As the founder of JD Consulting, she has helped numerous businesses to scale, create viral marketing campaigns and increase their brand visibility. Her innovative approach combines her business acumen with creative storytelling, making her a sought-after consultant for businesses looking to grow in the digital age.

In addition to her work in leadership and entrepreneurship, Dr Ducharme remains an active professor, continually shaping future leaders through education. She believes strongly in reinvesting in today's youth, understanding that they are the future of this world. Her contributions continue through her books, seminars and online content, where she provides thought leadership on topics like business strategy, leadership development, and female empowerment.

A sought-after speaker and advisor, Dr Ducharme continues to champion leadership and entrepreneurship, working tirelessly to inspire and empower others through her ventures, publications, and speaking engagements.

facebook.com/DrJulieDucharmeCOMMANDERINPINK
instagram.com/julietaylorducharme
linkedin.com/in/drjulieducharme
tiktok.com/@julietaylorducharme
facebook.com/DrJulieDucharmeCOMMANDERINPINK

KAREN PERKS

FINDING PEACE THROUGH STRUGGLE

Struggle is a word we don't like to sit with. It carries weight, heaviness, and sometimes even shame. But what if struggle wasn't weakness at all? What if it was strength in disguise – the slow layering of resilience, built one experience at a time.

I like to think of it as a raincoat. In the beginning, life gives us something light and flimsy – good enough for a drizzle but useless in a storm. Then the years add their weather. A disappointment here, a heartbreak there. The coat thickens. It begins to hold up in the wind. And one day, you find yourself standing in the middle of a downpour you thought would drown you, only to realise you're still standing. Not dry, not untouched; but stronger, shielded by all the layers of experience stitched together over time.

I remember when I was diagnosed with cardiomyopathy. Everything shifted. My values changed first – suddenly what mattered wasn't achievement or speed, but presence and health. Then my expectations changed, both of myself and of life. I could no longer live as if I had endless energy or time. That season taught me, in the hardest way, that struggle reshapes us. It strips away what is superficial and leaves us face-to-face with what really matters. In that struggle, I grew.

Peace, then, is not found in avoiding storms. It's found in knowing you've walked through them before, and you will again. This is what I wish to share: peace is not the absence of struggle, but what emerges when we learn to live within it. How it changes us with strength and empowerment to not suppress struggles but accept and even engage with our struggles to understand where our growth will take us.

UNDERSTANDING STRUGGLE AS STRENGTH

Looking back, some of the moments I thought would break me were actually the ones that built me. At the time, they felt like unbearable losses; the kind you believe no one could understand. But years later, I can see them differently. They didn't just leave scars; they stitched new layers of strength into me.

In my twenties, I thought resilience meant pretending I was fine. Smiling through the storm. Carrying on without asking for help. That version of strength looked good on the outside but left me soaked through on the inside. It took time, and more struggle than I'd like to admit, to learn that true strength is quieter. It's not about ignoring the storm; it's about learning how to walk through it with honesty, patience and eventually with grace.

One of the hardest storms I ever faced was the breakdown of my marriage. At the time, it felt like my world was collapsing. I was scared, ashamed and convinced I had failed, as a partner, as a woman and as a person. There were nights when I lay awake wondering if I would ever rebuild, or if I would always carry that sense of worthlessness. But slowly, through the tears and uncertainty, I began to realise that survival itself was strength. That loss was not the end of me, but the beginning of a new version of me.

Looking back now, I see how that storm stitched a new layer into my raincoat: courage. The courage to grow into changing situations. The courage to step forward when everything familiar had fallen away. The courage to believe that even broken pieces can be rebuilt into something stronger. That storm, as much as I once wished it had never come, gave me resilience I would carry into every struggle after.

Each challenge, whether it was loss, failure or heartbreak, became another layer of my raincoat. Thin at first, fragile even. But with every test, the fabric changed. It became tougher, more resilient, and able to withstand storms that once would have undone me. And that's the paradox of struggle: the very things we wish we could erase are often the things that equip us to keep going.

THE SANDBAGS OF LIFE

If the raincoat is about what we carry *through* storms, the hot air balloon is about what we carry *after* them. Imagine standing in the basket, ready to rise. Around you are sandbags. Some are heavy with fear, some stuffed with self-doubt, some filled with grief you never gave yourself permission to release.

The thing about sandbags is this: they serve two purposes. They can keep you safe, steady and close to the ground. Or they can hold you down, stopping you from rising into the life you're meant to live. The question is: which are yours doing?

For years, I carried sandbags I didn't even realise I had. Fear of failing. Fear of what people might think. Fear of letting go of an identity that no longer fit me. Those fears gave me a strange comfort because they kept me 'safe'. But they also kept me small. It wasn't until I started asking myself *what is this weight costing me?* that I began to cut a few ropes and let the balloon rise.

Sometimes we forget that sandbags aren't only a weight; they're also a stabiliser. In a real balloon, sandbags help to keep the basket steady in windy conditions, preventing it from tipping over. In the same way, some of the weights we carry serve a purpose. Our values, responsibilities and even certain fears can keep us grounded when life feels unpredictable.

Without them, we might drift too far, too fast, unanchored and unprepared. The wisdom lies in knowing which sandbags steady us and which ones simply keep us stuck on the ground.

One of the heaviest sandbags I carried for too long was the belief that I had to live up to an old version of myself. I clung to an identity that no longer served me, terrified of what it meant to outgrow it. That fear of failure, of stepping into something unknown, held me down far longer than I like to admit. Letting go of it didn't happen overnight; it took small, shaky steps, choosing every day to believe that I could rise even without the safety of what was familiar. When I finally cut that rope, I felt the shift. Not a sudden soaring, but a gentle lift, as though peace had been waiting, just beyond my fear, all along.

Of course, not all sandbags should be thrown overboard. Some ground us in the best ways: our values, our responsibilities, our sense of duty to those we love. But others? They keep us stuck in places we've outgrown. Letting go isn't always easy. But peace comes when you learn the difference between what keeps you safe and what keeps you stuck. Feel the power to cut those ropes that do not serve you.

CHOOSING PEACE

Peace is not something that arrives neatly wrapped when the storm ends. Peace is something we choose, often in the middle of the chaos itself. For a long time, I thought peace would come once the struggle was over. I kept waiting for that mythical 'after', where life would settle, and I could finally breathe. But life doesn't work like that. There is always another wave, another storm.

I remember one moment, sitting in a hospital room, surrounded by monitors and unanswered questions. The air was heavy with uncertainty. The diagnosis of cardiomyopathy had already shaken me, but in that sterile room, the reality of fragility became undeniable. My instinct was to fight it, to resist the fear and to demand control. I wanted answers, certainty – something to cling to. But somewhere in that long night, I realised I couldn't control the storm. I could only choose how to stand in it.

That moment changed me. I could either let the fear consume me, or I could find a different way of being within it. Choosing peace didn't mean pretending the illness wasn't real or ignoring how serious it was. It meant accepting that while I couldn't control the outcome, I could control how I carried myself through it. In that surrender, I found peace. Not because the struggle disappeared, but because I stopped fighting against its existence.

Peace, I've learned, isn't a finish line. It's a posture. Sometimes it means choosing freedom by cutting loose a sandbag that no longer serves you. Other times it means choosing safety by grounding yourself in what truly matters. Both can be peace, depending on the season. The trick is knowing which one your heart needs in that moment.

PRACTICAL PATHWAYS TO PEACE

Finding peace through struggle is not abstract, it's practical. It lives in small, ordinary choices that stack up to something extraordinary.

For me, one of those practices has been reframing the question. Instead of 'Why me?' I try to ask, 'What is this teaching me?' That shift didn't come naturally. In the beginning, I demanded answers. I wanted to know why I had to face illness, why my marriage had ended, why life felt so unfair. But over time, I learned that those questions left me stuck. When I changed the question, I began to see patterns – how struggle was teaching me courage, how loss was shaping empathy, and how illness was sharpening my values. That small change in language helped me make sense of pain in a way that built peace.

Gratitude has been another anchor. In the darkest moments, lying in hospital rooms or sitting in an empty house after my marriage ended, gratitude felt almost impossible. But I started with small things. A friend's message. A nurse's kindness. The sound of rain outside my window. They weren't solutions, but they were lifelines. Gratitude doesn't erase hardship, but it softens it. It makes space for peace to sit alongside pain. I remember one night in particular when I felt swallowed by fear, yet I wrote down three small things I was grateful for: the comfort of a blanket, a smile from a stranger and the strength to keep breathing. That list became a crack of light in a very dark room.

Journalling has also been one of my quiet tools. Putting words on paper allowed me to release what I couldn't always say aloud. Over time, those journals became proof of growth; I could trace the storms I thought I wouldn't survive and see how I had found my way through. Writing gave me perspective, and perspective gave me peace.

I've also leaned on rituals of letting go. One of the biggest was releasing the weight of perfectionism. I wrote down all the unrealistic expectations I was holding onto – being 'strong' all the time, never asking for help, always keeping it together – and burned the page. That act of release was simple but powerful. It gave me permission to be human, to admit vulnerability, and to rest. In letting go of those impossible standards, I found peace in my own imperfection.

Nature and movement have also become part of my healing rhythm. Walking outside, feeling the air on my skin and letting the world remind me of its beauty grounds me in ways nothing else can. When everything feels out of control, nature whispers of cycles, seasons and the quiet reassurance that storms always pass.

And finally, connection. Struggle can isolate us if we let it, but healing rarely happens alone. For me, peace has been found in the voices and presence of others, family, friends and communities that reminded me I wasn't carrying the weight by myself. Each conversation, each shared story, was like someone placing another stitch in my raincoat. Together, those connections created the fabric of peace that I couldn't have built on my own.

But there is another layer to connection: finding your tribe. When you change, not everyone comes with you. Some relationships belong to an older version of yourself, and holding onto them can feel like another kind of sandbag. I learned that when you grow through struggle, you often need to find new people, those who understand the person you are becoming, not just the person you were. My business community has been one of those tribes. They continue to give me strength and uplift me to levels I never expected. Being surrounded by people who believe in me and who encourage me to rise has become one of the most powerful pathways to peace in my life.

As I write these words, I think again of the raincoat and the balloon. One prepares you for the storm; the other lifts you when it passes. Together they tell the story of struggle and peace, how one shapes the other.

We don't get to choose whether the storms come. We don't always get to choose the sandbags life gives us. But we do get to choose how we carry them and when we let them go.

Peace, I've come to believe, isn't given. It's created. It's built layer by layer, storm by storm, release by release. Struggles are not punishments, they are teachers. And the more layers we stitch, the higher we rise.

If my life has taught me anything, it's that struggle will always leave its mark, but it also leaves us with new strength. My diagnosis, the breakdown of my marriage and the moments where fear felt heavier than hope, they didn't define me, but they refined me. They stripped away what didn't matter and revealed what did. And in that refining, I found peace. Not the kind that comes from a life without storms, but the kind that comes from knowing I can weather them.

Dolly Parton once sang of a 'Coat of Many Colours', stitched together with scraps but made priceless through love. In many ways, that is my life.

My raincoat of resilience is sewn from struggle, heartache and growth; each patch a story, each layer a lesson. It may not look perfect, but it carries me through storms and lifts me higher when the skies clear. That, to me, is peace; not something flawless or untouched, but something stitched together with love, courage and hope.

So here is the invitation: don't fear the storms. Don't cling to the sandbags that no longer serve you. Build your coat, release your weight and rise. Peace is waiting, not beyond the struggle, but within it.

ABOUT KAREN

Karen Perks is the CEO and founder of MiKare Health, a SaaS platform redefining how patients and carers engage with the health care system. A seasoned entrepreneur, author and strategic communications leader, Karen has built an international career across Australia and the UK. She now brings that expertise to driving MiKare's vision: restoring clarity, dignity and voice to people too often sidelined by fragmented systems.

For Karen, MiKare is deeply personal. After her daughter Mikayla was misdiagnosed by thirty doctors and endured more than two hundred seizures, Karen saw firsthand how badly communication breaks down between patients and professionals. That lived experience inspired both her memoir, *Mum, Please Help Me*, and her mission to reform health care so no family has to fight in silence.

Karen's leadership is defined by vision and execution. She combines commercial acumen with empathy, drawing on her background in strategic bid development, health communications and stakeholder engagement to turn lived stories into systemic change. She is also a published author, with projects such as the *Hear Us Roar* anthology series and a forthcoming Apple TV docufilm, reinforcing her commitment to amplifying unheard voices.

As a sought-after speaker, Karen has shared her story and insights on international stages – including at a castle in Ireland – where she inspired global audiences with her message of patient empowerment and systemic reform.

Through MiKare, Karen has positioned patient voice as a force for reform. She believes MiKare is more than a platform: it is a movement to give every patient their own health black box, a record that listens, remembers and ensures their voice is finally heard.

linkedin.com/in/karen-p-51253a57
instagram.com/karenperks_official
mikare.health

KAREN WEAVER
FINDING YOUR WAY BACK TO INNER PEACE

For this book, I really wanted to share a story of finding my way back to inner peace because life will always happen. We will always be thrown curveballs. We will be sent things that will shake us to our core, but it doesn't need to hit us at rock bottom. I want to share with you a few pivotal times in my life because I believe that sharing my story may resonate with you, and there's always something profound to learn from our deepest struggles. I'm sharing from a perspective of healing, of learning all the lessons life has taught me. I'm sharing from a perspective of hindsight, growth and profound transformation.

As an author of many books and a publisher, I believe deeply that we should journal whenever we are healing from something. When we actually come through difficult experiences and learn the lessons they offer, and when we get the call to share our stories, we should write them down so that other people can connect and begin their own healing journey. Our stories might ignite something within them, spark recognition or provide the hope they desperately need. I'm showing up here because I'm called to share my story, a few stories, actually, of when life threw me devastating curveballs and I had to find my way back to peace again.

KAREN WEAVER

UNDERSTANDING WHEN TO FIGHT AND WHEN TO FLOW

When something disturbs our peace or takes away our sense of stability, we must first determine if it's aligned with where we're going in life. If it's not aligned with our path and values, we have the power to dismiss it. We can choose not to engage. But if it's something connected to our core values, like our family, our health or our fundamental beliefs, something that we have to endure and can't avoid facing because we must come through it, then we cannot simply dismiss it. We have to do the inner work and come through it with intention and courage.

The beautiful truth I've discovered is that we will definitely emerge as a higher version of ourselves whenever we embrace these challenges and open our minds to the possibility that sometimes there's tremendous learning embedded in these experiences, as uncomfortable and painful as they may be in the moment.

THE FIRST FALL: WHEN EVERYTHING COLLAPSED (2006-2007)

The first time I was completely knocked off my perch was back in 2006. I had just given up a job that I absolutely loved, working as a tutor in special needs drama therapy. I was hired by a college to go out to various centres and deliver drama programs and other therapeutic interventions. I had also worked in mental health in an administrative role, but I was very much integrated into the whole treatment team and deeply involved in patient care. I observed so much during that time, learning about human resilience and the healing process, though I didn't realise how much that knowledge would serve me later.

I wasn't an author at this time. This was back in 2006, before I moved to Australia. I had just had my second son, and on the surface, life seemed good. But I was breastfeeding him, pouring every ounce of my energy into him, into my family, into everything and everyone around me. I had given up a career that fulfilled me deeply to focus entirely on motherhood. While I wasn't getting anything to fill my own cup, I was constantly giving, giving, giving, which is very much an Irish cultural expectation. Women in our culture are raised to sacrifice everything to be completely devoted to the home and family.

I had a partner who not only expected this total self-sacrifice but demanded it. The result was that I was miserable, and he was miserable too. Don't get me wrong, I love being a mother. It brings me immense joy and purpose. But every person needs something for themselves, something that lights them up and reminds them of who they are beyond their roles and responsibilities.

Life became increasingly difficult. Everything seemed to go wrong at once. The car would break down, money problems mounted and every day brought new challenges. Everything felt impossibly tough. I didn't know the things I know now about resilience, self-care and maintaining inner peace. I hadn't been through my spiritual awakening process yet and I was still very young and naive, around twenty-nine years old.

THE BREAKING POINT

When a particularly challenging incident happened in my home, something that shook me to my core, I realised I was teetering on the verge of that invisible line. You know the one I'm talking about, that line where if you drop below it, it becomes exponentially harder to climb back above it. I wasn't operating from a full cup; I was running on completely empty reserves.

Because I was operating from an empty cup, I had nothing, no reserves to pull from when this crisis hit. I sank like a stone. I hit absolute rock bottom and went into what I now recognise as post-traumatic stress.

My body would shake uncontrollably, I experienced tunnel vision and my capacity for handling even basic daily tasks became severely limited.

Today, I can fit enormous amounts into my day without feeling overwhelmed. I can feel in flow, balanced and capable of handling multiple complex situations simultaneously. But during that dark period, even just being the best mother I could be was all I had the capacity for each day. Nothing else and nobody else could enter the equation. That single focus, caring for my children, was literally all I could manage because motherhood is one of my highest values, and I had to pour everything I had left into that role.

THE COCOON PERIOD: 12-14 MONTHS OF SURVIVAL

This survival mode lasted for about twelve to fourteen months. I was deep in PTSD, just trying to get through each day. I called it my 'cocoon period' because I felt so raw and vulnerable, like I was wrapped in protective isolation while trying to heal. During this time, I felt emotions toward another human being that I never thought I was capable of feeling, dark, heavy emotions that scared me.

I was incredibly stubborn about getting help, but luckily, having worked in mental health, I understood what was happening to me. I didn't like it, but I could recognise the symptoms and the process. I was absolutely determined not to become a statistic, not to end up medicated and dependent on pharmaceutical solutions alone. I decided to do the deep inner work that I knew was necessary for real healing.

THE DOUBLE LOSS THAT BECAME A BLESSING

During this period of emotional numbness and survival mode, I experienced a double miscarriage. When you're in post-traumatic stress, you become very numb to life, you're disconnected from your emotions as a protective mechanism. Knowing what I know now about the law of attraction, gratitude and the fundamental laws of nature, I understand that I wasn't in a state to attract positive experiences into my life. I was caught in what felt like a negative vortex, suspended in limbo where nothing good seemed to happen.

When I discovered I was pregnant with twins, it was like a brilliant light had suddenly appeared in my world. I felt happiness and joy for the first time in over a year. Even though I hadn't been trying to conceive, these babies came as a beautiful surprise that filled me with hope and reminded me that life could still hold wonder and beauty.

Then, just one week after that joyful discovery, I started to lose them. I lost one first, then the other. I remember lying there praying desperately to save even one baby, drawing on my mother's experience, she had lost a twin when carrying my sister. I held onto hope and prayed with everything I had left.

But I remember the exact moment when I felt something shift in my body, a definitive 'pop', and I knew with absolute certainty that the second baby was gone. I cried with a depth and intensity I had never experienced before. The tears felt like they were coming from the deepest part of my soul. I cried and cried and cried until I had what I can only describe as flood tears.

In retrospect, I realise I wasn't just crying for the loss of those precious babies; I was also crying for the time I had lost to PTSD, for the woman I had been before who seemed to have disappeared entirely. But within this profound grief came an unexpected blessing: I was feeling again.

THE AWAKENING: FEELING AGAIN

I had always been someone who could walk into a room and light it up. I was the life and soul of every party, vibrant and full of energy. But during my PTSD period, I had become numb to life, just a shadow of my former self, going through the motions without any real presence or joy. There was none of the essential 'me' left anymore.

Through the grief of losing the twins, I began to feel again. This return to emotional awareness became the catalyst for my healing journey. In that moment of profound loss and pain, I made three sacred promises to myself that would become the foundation of my recovery and transformation.

THREE SACRED PROMISES

First, I decided I was no longer going to care about what anybody else thought of me. I realised that everyone else's opinion is truly none of my business. This wasn't about becoming callous or inconsiderate; it was about freeing myself from the exhausting burden of trying to meet everyone else's expectations at the expense of my own wellbeing.

Second, I acknowledged that I'm naturally ambitious and love achieving meaningful goals. I committed to go after what I truly wanted in life, to trust my instincts completely and to embark on what I called a 'joy ride' of authentic living. Moreover, I promised to share what I learned and show other people how they could do the same, how they could reclaim their authentic selves and pursue their dreams fearlessly.

Third, and perhaps most importantly, I vowed that I would never allow myself to go below that line again. I committed to maintaining a higher vibration, to staying in love with life and to keeping my cup full so that I could weather future storms without losing myself completely.

Once I made this fundamental shift and committed to this new path, something magical began to happen. Wise messages started coming my way. Insights and wisdom flowed to me in ways that absolutely blew my mind, and I became incredibly receptive to this guidance.

THE BACKYARD PEACE PROJECT: VOL 1

THE FLOW RETURNS

Everything started to align once I made this switch to what I knew was the right path for my life. We received our visas to Australia, something we'd been working toward for years. I became pregnant again almost immediately, this time with a healthy pregnancy. We successfully immigrated to the other side of the world, starting fresh in a new country. Money began to flow more easily, opportunities opened up and everything started moving in positive directions again.

Most importantly, I was genuinely happy, happier than I had been in years. The contrast between this period and those dark few years of struggle was absolutely remarkable. I had learned viscerally how crucial it is to maintain your inner reserves and keep your cup full.

THE SECOND TEST: MY DAUGHTER'S HEALTH CRISIS (2023)

That first experience taught me invaluable lessons about resilience and self-care, but life had another major test in store for me. In 2023, my daughter, who was thirteen years old at the time, was diagnosed with type 1 diabetes. This story provides a powerful contrast to my first experience because it shows how differently we can handle crises when we're operating from a place of inner strength rather than depletion.

We didn't initially know what was wrong with her. She had always been a child who caught viruses easily, tonsillitis, various infections and always ran high temperatures. But this time was distinctly different, and my maternal instincts were screaming that something was seriously wrong.

I had to rush her to the emergency room late at night because I was genuinely frightened for her life. She couldn't even walk properly and kept collapsing. When we arrived at the hospital, I witnessed something

I'd never seen before. She was taken into the ICU faster than I thought was humanly possible. There were ambulances everywhere, no waiting in the emergency room. She was brought straight in because her organs were actually beginning to fail due to ketosis, and she had lost a dramatic amount of weight seemingly overnight.

The medical team immediately pumped her full of glucose and other medications to stabilise her blood sugar levels. It was absolutely shocking to witness how quickly she had deteriorated and how efficiently the medical team had to work to save her life. After about a week of intensive treatment, we finally got her stabilised and began to understand what we were dealing with.

THE GREATER CHALLENGE: OCD

For my needle-phobic daughter, the transition to requiring five insulin injections daily, plus constant finger pricks for blood sugar monitoring, was already a monumental adjustment. But what proved to be even more challenging was the OCD that developed about six months after her diabetes diagnosis. This condition completely consumed her life and, by extension, our entire family's life.

My daughter is my fourth child out of six, and she came into our lives just after I lost the twins I mentioned earlier. She has always held a special place in my heart. But the difference in how I handled this crisis compared to my earlier breakdown was night and day, and it all came down to one crucial factor: I intentionally kept my cup full throughout this ordeal.

Because I was maintaining a high vibration and had learned to care for myself properly, I had the emotional, physical and spiritual strength to pour into her when she needed me most. She desperately needed her mother to be strong, present and capable, and I was able to show up for her in that way because I had maintained my reserves.

When her OCD reached its peak, she would shower for hours and hours at a time. I would have to coach her through each episode, talking her through her anxiety and compulsions with patience and understanding. This condition literally consumed my life for extended periods. My business began to suffer significantly, and I had several frustrated authors whose projects were delayed, which was completely understandable given the circumstances.

But I had to make the choice to prioritise saving my child's life and supporting her healing. I couldn't simply hand her care over to someone else because her situation was more complex than standard treatment protocols could address. Additionally, we were dealing with all of this during the height of COVID restrictions, which complicated access to various forms of support and treatment.

THE LONG JOURNEY TO HEALING

I knew instinctively that I was the right person to support her through this challenging period, and we worked together on her healing for years. There were multiple rock bottom moments where she needed intensive support, times when her OCD escalated to new levels of severity. She even required surgery at one point because she developed an abscess from repeated insulin injections in the same area, a physical manifestation of the psychological compulsions she was battling.

Throughout all of this, I had to pour enormous amounts of energy, attention and emotional resources into her care. The crucial difference from my earlier crisis was that I could sustain this level of giving because I was simultaneously taking care of myself and keeping my own cup full. I maintained my reserve tank of emotional and spiritual resources.

My sister, Emma Weaver from Mental Wealth International, talks about the importance of keeping your 'mental wealth bank' filled so that when you need to tap into your resources during life's inevitable challenges, you have substantial reserves available. I certainly drew heavily on those reserves during my daughter's health crisis, but because I had built them up intentionally, I was able to weather the storm without losing myself.

Today, I'm thrilled to report that my daughter is thriving. She's doing remarkably well, managing her diabetes effectively and her OCD is under control. We survived one of the most challenging periods of our lives together, and we both emerged stronger.

THE CRUCIAL CONTRAST

I cannot overstate how important it is for me to share these two stories in direct contrast to each other. What happened with my daughter, a life-threatening medical condition followed by a severe mental health crisis, was objectively more serious and complex than the initial incident that sent me into PTSD years earlier.

Yet that first, arguably less severe, situation took far more out of me and resulted in complete breakdown, PTSD and over a year of survival mode living. The reason for this dramatic difference wasn't the severity of the external circumstances; it was entirely about where I was personally and the environment I had created in my life.

During the first crisis, I was operating from complete depletion, had no support systems in place and hadn't developed the tools and wisdom necessary to maintain my wellbeing during difficult times. During my daughter's health crisis, even though we were dealing with more serious medical and psychological challenges, I was able to handle everything more effectively because I had learned to keep my cup full and maintain my inner reserves.

THE ESSENTIAL TRUTH ABOUT SELF-CARE

This contrast illustrates why it's absolutely crucial for us to ensure that we're keeping our cup full to overflowing at all times. We must make it a priority to pour into ourselves, to stop and take time for our own needs and to engage in activities that keep us at a higher vibration and maintain our inner peace.

When we do this consistently, when life inevitably happens, and it always will happen because we are human beings living full, complex lives, it might knock us over a little bit, but it won't sink us to rock bottom. We won't lose ourselves completely in the crisis because we've maintained our core strength and identity.

A MESSAGE OF HOPE AND EMPOWERMENT

I sincerely hope that sharing these intimate and sometimes painful stories will truly help someone who needs to hear them today. I hope they reach the heart and mind of someone who feels overwhelmed, depleted or lost in their own challenges. I want you to feel supported, motivated and deeply understood.

Most importantly, I want you to really grasp that taking care of yourself and pursuing what brings you joy and fulfilment is not selfish, it's an absolute priority. When you put yourself first and foremost, you become infinitely more capable of supporting the people around you effectively.

Your children will benefit enormously from seeing you model healthy self-care. They will learn not to sacrifice all of themselves for others, but rather to put themselves first so they can show up fully for the people they love. This is one of the greatest gifts you can give them, the example of someone who knows their worth and maintains their wellbeing.

When you have a full cup, you're able to pour generously into others, and it becomes a beautiful, sustainable cycle. Instead of sacrificing all of yourself as a mother, as a leader in your family, as a professional or community member, you can show up as your best self because you've taken care of your own needs first.

Your children and their children will learn from this powerful example that you take care of yourself because it's important. After all, you matter, and when you take care of yourself, everyone else around you benefits immeasurably. This is how we break generational patterns of depletion and sacrifice, and how we model what it looks like to live a life of sustainable joy, purpose and service to others.

ABOUT KAREN

K P Weaver is a visionary author, accomplished publisher and life philosopher known for her profound insights into mindfulness, knowing, intention, love, gratitude, forgiveness and belief. With a remarkable career spanning various genres, including novels, motivational literature, children's books and journals, she has consistently led the way in her authorship, generously sharing her transformative philosophies through the power of the written word.

Her journey is a testament to the boundless potential of human existence. As an award-winning author and a TEDx speaker, she has penned numerous books and touched the hearts and minds of readers worldwide. Her work transcends traditional literary boundaries, offering profound wisdom and guidance in diverse facets of life.

In addition to her prolific writing career, Karen has emerged as a prominent figure in the publishing world. Having built a highly successful publishing empire from the ground up, she has nurtured major authors, authored over forty impactful books, and established her own credible brand in the market. Her innovative strategies and techniques are anchored in the power of 'knowing' to manifest dreams and aspirations into reality.

A recognised, gifted teacher who inspires others to harness the magic of life, she imparts her transformative wisdom through her seven life principles, each a masterful element in her journey to success. These principles serve as a guiding light, illuminating the path to personal growth, fulfilment and achievement. Her biggest call to action was to awaken those who sleep, through the power of story.

Her life philosophy revolves around the idea that when mindfulness, intention, love, gratitude, forgiveness and belief converge at the right time and circumstance, true magic happens. Her life and work stand as a testament to the boundless potential that resides within each of us.

kpwofficial.com

KATHERINE MCLEOD

THE LIFE I CHOSE
THE MOMENT THAT CHANGED EVERYTHING

It was 2016, and I remember the moment like it was yesterday. My assistant, Sandra, said goodbye at the end of a regular workday – only, she never came back. She died suddenly, not long after. She was just fifty. Vivacious. Kind. Caring. The most loved member of staff. Her presence lit up the whole place.

Her passing shattered something in me. She was full of life, joy and purpose … and just like that, she was gone. It was terrifying. It made me question everything – my choices, my direction, the life I was living.

That moment cracked me open.

It was the first time I truly realised: life could end in an instant. And I was not living mine fully. I was achieving, yes, and succeeding, yes. But inside, I was disconnected from the deep fulfilment I craved.

A year later, I followed the quiet nudge within and attended a retreat on the Sunshine Coast. It changed me. For the first time in years, I felt truly at peace. I felt myself exhale. I was no longer chasing something outside of me.

It was there, surrounded by stillness and soul-nourishing space, that I saw the truth: **I had been living someone else's dream.**

And I was done with that.

I made a choice that day to no longer pursue external success at the cost of my soul. To finally explore the question: *What would it mean to live a life that is mine?*

THE BEFORE: CHASING ENOUGHNESS

Before that moment of awakening, my life was built around effort. I made everything hard. I was the one who stayed back late, working until 1am to get everything just right. I was always striving to prove something, to fix everything, to show everyone just how capable I was. I carried the identity of a problem-solver. A high-achiever with a growth mindset. The dependable one.

But underneath all of that was a deeper truth I wasn't ready to admit: I didn't feel like I was enough.

So I kept trying to compensate.

I worked harder than everyone else. I went above and beyond because I needed it to mean something. I needed *me* to mean something.

At the time, I was working as a special-needs teacher. I was good at it – really good, actually. But what I didn't see clearly then was how detrimental it had become to my wellbeing. The constant alertness, the daily problem-solving, the emotional energy it required – it left very little of *me* for *me*.

I was constantly in a heightened state of tension, emotionally and physically. It was like I couldn't exhale. I'd go home each night and drink a bottle of champagne just to come down from the day. And even then, I'd lie in bed wondering: *Is this it? Is this what I'm here for?*

Sandra's death shook me, not just because of the loss, but because she was the mirror I didn't know I needed. Her life – joyful, connected and free – contrasted with everything I had been doing. She didn't try to prove her worth. She just *was*. Loved. Enough. Present.

She woke me up to the truth: All this striving wasn't leading to fulfilment – it was hiding from it.

And I knew, deep down, something had to change.

THE TURNING POINT: WHAT IF I COULD CHOOSE?

THE BACKYARD PEACE PROJECT: VOL 1

Sandra's death woke something up in me that I couldn't put back to sleep.

It asked questions I had never really let myself ask: Am I truly happy with the life I'm living? What if my life ended tomorrow – would I feel fulfilled? What if I could choose differently … right now?

That question haunted and liberated me all at once. I began to wonder: Could I really choose a new life? One that I actually enjoyed? One that felt exciting, soulful, and real?

The possibility cracked me open. And I followed it.

I booked a retreat. I invested $10,000 for a single week – an amount that, at the time, felt like a wild leap. But it also felt like a line in the sand. I wasn't buying a holiday. I was choosing myself for the first time in a long time.

That decision marked the beginning of everything.

The retreat was life-altering. For the first time, I stepped away from the constant noise of responsibility and into sacred space. Space to think, feel, reflect and just be. And in that space, I discovered a different version of myself – one I hadn't met before.

I returned from that retreat a different woman. More aware. More conscious. Lighter, brighter and somehow more grounded than ever before.

It wasn't that all my problems disappeared – it's that I was no longer trying to prove my worth through fixing them.

I no longer wanted to be the woman who lived on autopilot. I was no longer satisfied with surviving. I wanted to create. I wanted to choose. I wanted to feel alive.

Sandra's passing was the catalyst. The retreat was the container. And my yes was the turning point.

Everything began to change from that moment forward – not all at once, but deeply and undeniably.

KATHERINE MCLEOD

THE JOURNEY: RELEASING WHAT WAS NEVER MINE

When I returned home from the retreat, people noticed something right away.

'You look different,' they said. And I *was* different.

I wasn't jumpy anymore. I wasn't micromanaging or snapping at everyone. I wasn't forcing or pushing or controlling everything around me.

It was the first time in my life that I felt still. Present. And it showed.

That retreat didn't just change my perspective – it cracked open a lifetime of unprocessed emotion and coping strategies I had mistaken for personality.

In those sacred few days away, I came face to face with three core wounds that had quietly run my life for decades.

1. Control I had been controlling everything – my environment, my to-do list, other people's reactions – because I didn't feel safe unless I did. Letting go of control wasn't just an idea. It was a full-body release. My hands shook. My chest trembled. My entire nervous system responded like it was being rewired. Because it was. For the first time, I wasn't the woman holding it all together – and I didn't fall apart. I softened.
2. Anger I had always seen anger as dangerous, messy and wrong. As a child, I never allowed myself to express it. I became 'the good girl' – agreeable, compliant, never angry. But that anger didn't go away. It turned inward. It became resentment, self-pressure and perfectionism. At the retreat, I met that rage head-on – and I let it rise. It was terrifying and liberating. And in expressing it, I finally reclaimed parts of myself I hadn't allowed to exist.
3. Grief, this was the emotion I had buried deepest. The sadness of Sandra's death. The grief I never voiced for other losses. I had thought grieving was weak. That being seen crying meant I had lost control.

But when I finally let myself cry – truly, uncontrollably cry – it wasn't weakness. It was a release. I wasn't breaking down. I was letting go.

During one of the processes at the retreat, my body went into full convulsions. It was like a dam bursting. Decades of emotional holding cracked open. My nervous system had been locked in hypervigilance – always alert, always braced. And for the first time, it exhaled.

I remember people watching me in awe. They could see the shift happening in real time – the physical release of tension that had been holding me hostage my whole life. It was wild. It was sacred. It was real healing.

And when I returned home, I wasn't the same.

My family and I had to reacquaint ourselves with one another. They were used to the high-achieving, controlling, fast-talking version of me. Now, I was softer. More grounded. More present. And for the first time in my life, I wasn't trying to make anyone else different.

I allowed them to be themselves. Because I was finally allowing *myself* to be me.

I had found the woman beneath the constant need to prove something. And she was whole.

THE TRANSFORMATION: A NEW INNER WORLD

Life feels worlds apart from what it once was.

Where there was once tension, there is now lightness. Where there was once self-judgement, there is now support. My inner voice – once sharp, critical and relentless – is now gentle, curious and encouraging. I finally feel free on the inside. And that freedom has changed everything.

I used to live with constant insecurity. Always blaming myself. Always questioning if I was too much or not enough. But now? I like who I am. Actually, I love who I am.

I feel at home in my skin. I know what I stand for. I lead with love.

And I find immense joy in lighting that spark in others.

My mission is to lead, love, and leave a legacy – and it no longer feels like a burden or something I need to prove. It's a natural expression of who I've become.

These days, I smile more. I laugh a lot. I'm bolder, more daring, more direct – but with a softness that welcomes people in. I don't get offended the way I used to. I don't need everyone to agree with me. I can hold different opinions with grace.

And most of all, I feel safe to be seen. To speak up. To stand in front of a room and share my mission to empower women, to help them remember their magic, come home to their worth, and create lives that overflow with joy, creativity, and freedom.

That's the thing about transformation: It doesn't just change how you *feel*. It changes what you *do* – and how you do it.

A year after that life-changing retreat, I gave birth to my beautiful daughter, Penelope. She arrived earthside as if to reflect the woman I had become – light-filled, soulful, magical. Her presence has been an unexpected but perfect part of my journey.

Because in giving birth to her, I experienced a rebirth of myself. And now, at fifty-one, I feel more alive, more fulfilled and more in love with life than ever before.

Penelope is joy embodied – and having her in my life is a daily reminder of what truly matters: Presence. Love. And being fully, unapologetically *you*.

This is what freedom feels like. And I wouldn't trade it for anything.

A MESSAGE TO YOU, DEAR READER

If there's one message I could pass on with all the love and wisdom I've gathered, it's this:

You are far more powerful than you realise. And your life – your sacred, one-of-a-kind life – is yours to create.

Everything begins with awareness. Noticing the patterns. Becoming conscious of the ways you hold yourself back, especially in the exact places you long to move forward. Often, we avoid the very thing we desire most – not because we don't want it, but because we're loyal to old stories, family patterns or the fear of being too different … too big … too free.

But true belonging doesn't come from staying small. It comes from being *real*.

This is the quiet revolution. The liberation. To live a life that's designed by *you*, not just inherited from someone else's expectations.

Life is short. It is precious. And you deserve to love your life – to fill it with joy, with soul, with play and with the people who light you up.

You don't have to do it alone. Sometimes all it takes is one person to help you see clearly. To walk beside you as you cross the bridge from the life you were handed … to the one you *choose*.

So here's my wish for you: Live a life you love, with people you love, doing what you love, in the way that *you* love it.

Because it's *yours*.

ABOUT KATHERINE

Katherine M McLeod is the visionary founder of the Divine Woman Experience, a transformative movement redefining self-worth and empowerment for women worldwide. From her soulful retreats to her revolutionary Self Worth RESET, Katherine inspires women to rise into their highest potential, blending the art of feminine leadership with the science of deep personal transformation. Her work has ignited profound shifts in health, wealth and relationships for countless women, proving that when you align with your magic, the extraordinary becomes inevitable. As a heart-led global impact leader, Katherine's mission is clear: to illuminate the path for women to create lives of purpose, abundance and unapologetic joy.

Divine Woman Experience Page
facebook.com/groups/598773588279579

Divine Manifesting Masterclass page
facebook.com/groups/652691360528659

LAURA MUIRHEAD
WHAT I FOUND IN THE REMAINS

Peace can come from someone's words.

I know this is true. A simple sentence, 'Pay attention to what remains,' brought me peace even as I stood across the street from my dream house in my nightgown, watching the flames engulf it.

I was the one who called the fire department. Somehow, I had managed to grab my phone from the nightstand when I was startled awake by the shouts of my husband that the house was on fire. Even in my dazed, half-awake state, I had the presence of mind to dial emergency to report the fire. I saw the flames outside our bedroom window as I rushed downstairs.

Phone in hand, I looked around the kitchen for the source of the fire. The shock of the moment clouded my logic. The fire was still outside on the back deck for a few more minutes.

My husband quickly freed our puppy from her crate. She ran to me and I scooped her up into my arms. Another one of our dogs came along with me to the front door. I was able to grab a leash and my sweatshirt jacket as a second makeshift leash. In that short time, the fire had begun to burst through the windows on the back of the house, setting off the smoke alarms. With the sirens blaring and my husband yelling to get out of the house, our third dog ran back upstairs, quickly followed by my husband. There was no way he was going to leave her.

At the top of the stairs, he called to her, begging her to please come to him. As he took another breath, he realised the oxygen was gone from the air. Luckily, she did run back to him.

The chill of the October morning didn't register. We corralled our dogs temporarily in our car on the driveway.

Dan, in his night clothes and barefoot, ran next door to wake our neighbour.

It was about that time that Dan saw the explosion from the propane tank on our back deck. His sense of urgency was even more heightened.

Just as Dan was pounding on the front door, the police arrived, helping our elderly neighbor and his dog escape their house.

The police moved us across the street to another neighbour's driveway. My three dogs and I were temporarily sardined in the back seat of the back seat of a police cruiser. If you've never had the pleasure of riding in the back of a police car, let me assure you, there is no legroom, even for my short legs. When you add three Labrador retrievers to that space, it is quite crowded and not extremely comfortable. Even so, I was relieved to have the warmth of the car.

We were surprised to discover that our neighbours were home. They graciously invited us in, freeing me from the discomfort of the backseat. Our dogs were safe in their garage. I was grateful when they dug in their closet to find some clothes for me to wear. Even if it was a mismatched top and lounge pants with flip-flops, it was better than my nightgown and bare feet. I was grateful.

This had all been a flurry of activity. After the police, the fire trucks arrived. I anxiously watched out the windows as the fire continued across the street. Why was it taking so long for the fireman to get set up?

At some point, I sent a message to my brand-new mentor to let her know I was going to have to reschedule our first session. This was her response:

'Pay attention to what remains.'

Those words changed everything for me. They immediately gave me a sense of presence in the moment and moved my mindset. I had also recently begun an online program focused on money mindset. Of course, that radiates out to change more than just your mindset around money. It had already begun to transform me in other ways.

One of the things I had hoped would remain was our house.

In my mind, the firemen would show up and quickly be able to extinguish the fire. That changed as I saw the flames break through the windows on the front of our house. Knowing that the fire started at the back of our house, seeing the front also engulfed in flames was the moment I knew that our house would not, in fact, be something that remained.

Still, over the next days, weeks and months, I did focus on what remained.

We remained, our dogs remained. The day after the fire, when my husband and the insurance adjuster were back to have a look at our house, our cat was discovered in the wet soot and ashes. Dan rushed her to the veterinarian. After a thorough exam and a bath, she was fortunately absolutely fine and back with the attitude we know and love.

There were definitely things to be grateful for. My two-week-old car was parked in our garage. I thought that the keys were most likely in my purse (which had burned, but somehow my singed wallet was found along with my partially melted driver's license). Miraculously, my son discovered that the keys were actually in the car. Somehow, they had fallen out of my purse a few days before the house fire. After a cleanup by the car dealership to remove the smell of smoke, we were obviously happy to have use of that car.

My husband's car, on the other hand, had to be towed and new keys made. Again, we were grateful that it also survived the fire.

We moved into a long-term hotel. It was two bedrooms with a living room and a kitchenette. I call it our three-room mansion, happy to have it for an intermediary home.

Even so, you can imagine it wasn't an ideal situation for two adults, three dogs and a cat. The dog walking alone was time-consuming. We were very conscious of the fact that every door closing in the parking lot outside our windows would potentially set off a barking session if we were not 'home' with our dogs.

Our son and his fiancée were enlisted to help dog sit while we began to re-establish our lives.

Keep in mind that we own a business that we continued to run on a daily basis. On the afternoon of the fire, our first stop was the mall, not only for essentials like clothes and shoes, but a computer and the necessities for me to work from my new home office at the hotel.

What a sight we must have been walking into the mall, though. No doubt, there must have been a faint scent of smoke wafting around us. Plus our borrowed clothes and shoes. Luckily, I had my melted but readable driver's license, so the store clerk was able to look up my credit card for payment.

I had fortunately grabbed my phone, but Dan needed to replace his. We needed to get things that we tend to take for granted. Hair brushes, a hairdryer, tooth brushes, toothpaste, etc. It wasn't until after my first shower in the hotel that I realised I had forgotten to buy a comb.

Top of our list was clearly to find a rental house. Our insurance company was helping with this, but we also took this matter into our own hands to expedite the search. Because of our action, we moved out of the three-room mansion after what seemed like the longest month of our lives.

Another lesson learned during that time was the grace of receiving.

On the morning of the fire, we were able to find a safe stopover at my brother-in-law's house. While Dan spent time with the insurance adjuster at our house, I made phone calls. One call was to notify my best friend in California about the fire. She offered to fly out to help, but still in shock, I told her I didn't see any possible way she could help us. Fortunately for us, she didn't listen to me. As I was laying my head down on the hotel pillow that night, I received a text message from her. 'I'll be there at 7:30 tomorrow morning.'

Thank goodness for her. She helped me cancel and replace credit cards and call the utility companies, thinking of things that I didn't have the brain space for, and taking detailed notes that I relied on months later. She was there to support us and even laugh with us at times. You can't place a value on having the kind of peace a good friend offers in those situations.

Over the next few months, we moved forward day by day. During the months we spent in the rental house, we replaced our belongings. The decision was made not to rebuild our house but to buy a different house. Eight months after our house burned, we moved into our new home.

It has been quite a few years since then. Looking back, I know that opportunities opened up for us that wouldn't have presented themselves had we stayed in that house.

We purchased a second house in another state. That led to me discovering a passion and talent for working with clay and creating ceramics. I opened a pottery/art studio near our second home and ran it for five years. Even though I've moved on to other projects, I am so grateful for the time and opportunity to grow from that experience.

The decision to close my studio came at a time when my path was shifting again. I didn't have to close it; I made the choice to do it to make more space for my next chapter. Literally, I began to write and share my stories.

One book led to another. Invitations arrived for speaking, collaborating and connecting with people around the world. I never could have imagined that losing our home would eventually lead me here, to this work, this voice and this version of myself.

I firmly believe that every twist and turn in the road is an opportunity to learn, grow and evolve. It is the overarching theme of my life and why my memoir is titled *A Funny Thing Happened on the Way to My Life*. It is the mindset, the perspective you bring when faced with life's challenges that makes all the difference. Finding gratitude in each and every one of them is a game-changer.

We were never going to have a victim attitude after our house burned to the ground. Sure, that seemingly simple sentence helped me to reframe things, but we knew the only course of action was to move forward, one step at a time, one day at a time. Having gratitude for what remained and being open to new possibilities and opportunities also helped to support us on our journey.

Finally telling my story, being authentic to myself and my voice, has been an important step in bringing peace to my soul. I am continually surprised and amazed at the things that are presented in my path because of the decision to write about parts of my life that I held back for so long.

We've built a life that we love beyond the flames. Our business is thriving, and every area of my life feels abundant, personally, professionally and spiritually. We've created a life that offers freedom and is fulfilling. I'm grateful every day for what we've built, what we've learned and most of all, for who we've become along the way.

Peace, for me, isn't about everything being calm or perfect. It's about being honest with myself, trusting the path and showing up authentically, no matter what life brings. And from where I stand now, I can see that what remained was more than enough.

I encourage you to find peace, no matter what unexpected challenges life might present. Again, it can be found in a single, simple sentence, in words that land just right in the moment and can shift everything. It can be found in looking for the gratitude of everyday life and especially in the twists and turns along the way. There can be incredible opportunities that show up on the other side, sometimes ones you never imagined could happen.

You might even find that peace was there all along, and that it always shows up in what remains.

ABOUT LAURA

Laura Muirhead is an internationally acclaimed author, speaker and the CFO of her family's multimillion-dollar company. She is also the creator of the Queen Code program and Queen Code Oracle Card Deck, a body of work designed to help women find clarity, honour their boundaries and elevate both their personal and professional lives. Laura's story is one of resilience, reinvention and healing. After navigating unexpected twists, including rebuilding her life after a devastating house fire, she has turned her experiences into guiding lights for others seeking peace and transformation. She is the author of *A Funny Thing Happened on the Way to My Life*, a number-one bestselling memoir, as well as a children's book and three reflective journals. A multi-passionate creator and healer, Laura bridges the worlds of business and soul work, showing that strength and compassion can coexist. She cherishes time with her husband, grown children, close friends and her Labrador retriever, while splitting her time between homes in New Jersey and Michigan. Her life reflects a devotion to creativity, adventure and a deep belief in the ripple effect of choosing peace.

afunnythinghappenedonthewaytomylife.com

LINDA PIERSON
THIS IS WHO I AM IN THE WORLD ...

I have an adventurous spirit that is most satisfied when I'm discovering something new or travelling and immersing myself in the local culture, food and music, and genuinely connecting to people. By nature, I'm very curious. My mum once told me that she was very sure that my third word spoken as a child was 'why', and I continued to ask why until I had gathered enough information that had satisfied my curiosity and understanding. I know it was very frustrating for such young parents; mum often shared stories of things I had asked perfect strangers, out of the blue, which left her bewildered and sometimes a little embarrassed. My natural disposition to be curious is something that serves me well in my chosen profession now.

I have and always had a genuine love for people; my life experiences have shaped my beliefs that we are all here to have numerous human experiences and ultimately to navigate our way through our challenges and create a life of joy.

I am the child of a Greek/French mother born in Jerusalem – who was one of thousands refugeed to France in 1957 following World War II – and an orphaned French father. Both of my parents came from poor and dysfunctional families, yet they made a choice to create a different life for themselves and their family.

In 1969, my parents migrated to Australia; they were only twenty-two and twenty-seven with two children in tow – I was five and my brother was four. We arrived in December, and I started school the following February. My mum had me all dressed up like Shirley Temple as she would have in Paris, with my little tin lunch box, black patent shoes and curls in my hair. I arrived at a school full of kids wearing shorts, T-shirts and many with bare feet. You can imagine how I stood out like a sore thumb, and the locals did not like what they saw.

I couldn't speak English, so I was unable to understand the insults, but the tone and facial expressions said it all, and on the third day of school, a few kids thought it would be funny to throw rocks at me on my way home. Seven stitches later – and what I can only imagine was an enraged interaction between my dad, who spoke little English and the school principal – the principal decided in his wisdom to keep me in during recess and lunchtime for an entire year for my own protection! Yep, the weird kid was now ostracised and segregated from the rest of the kids. But there was a gift thanks to the most beautiful person, Mrs Faulton, who came in with me every day during recess and lunchtime for that whole year. She taught me to speak English, she was open to all my 'why' questions and would happily answer, and she would bring me books on the subject I had queries about, and if she didn't know the answer, we'd research together.

I guess for me this was the beginning of understanding that one person can make a difference, there are good people in the world. People will always act at their worst when they make decisions from a place of fear, beliefs can be changed, and everything in life is a choice. My dad taught me how to box and told me I was never allowed to start a fight, but I was never to come home crying if I lost a fight. This led to me becoming the bully's bully.

Imagine this, I'm seven and out of solitary confinement; a new year. I'm dressed more like the locals, wearing jeans and a T-shirt. It was my first day back at school after the holidays, and the leader of the bullies with her little posse behind them cornered me in the toilets. Remember, my dad taught me to box, I quietly wanted her to hit me or push me so I could get my revenge! She asked me what was in my lunch box, she called me a wog and she told me I smelled, but I needed her to be physical because I wasn't allowed to throw the first punch. After a round of insults, with it looking like nothing further would happen, I decided to leave, and that's when she grabbed me and pushed me back into the toilet block. I told her not to touch me (Dad also said, 'Take out the leader and then ask who is next.'), giving her a second chance, but she grabbed me. So I turned around and punched her out and then stood there and said, 'Right, who's next?'

That moment felt amazing, but that was the beginning of my reputation. I became who I thought I should be: the bully's bully, the kid you wanted to beat in a fight to be known as the tough kid. Every day I was in fights; every day I'd have some little kid come up to me and tell me someone was picking on them, and I made it my business to take care of their business. This reputation followed me through primary school into high school. I was sixteen and a half when I decided I didn't want this, I didn't want to be this person, but I didn't know how to stop! I wasn't sure how to turn things around. Then one day I thought, what if I let someone just beat me up, then they could become the top dog? Then I could start being who I wanted to be!

I loved drama and art, I loved geography, and I loved learning, but these daily fights were not pleasant, and going to school sucked. A new student – let's call her Joanne – came to our school after being expelled from two other schools. She was looking for me and found me in the toilets. She asked if I knew Linda Pierson. I said, 'NAH.' I wasn't ready for the beating. A few days later, there was a crowd of kids hanging around the gymnasium after school. I asked some kids, 'What's going on?'

One kid said, 'Linda Pierson and that new chick, Joanne, are having a punch on.'

I said, 'Oh, interesting,' and tried to slink my way around the crowd to go home because once again, I wasn't ready for a beating. However, someone pointed me out in the crowd and Joanne came and pulled my hair. I thought, 'Okay, today's the day. Today you lose the title of "the tough kid you've gotta beat".' So I told Joanne that she scared me, that she was much tougher than me, but she wanted the drama. She wanted the spectacle. She wanted the fight.

I walked away twice and each time she pulled my hair, but when I turned around, she was just mouthy and only pushing and shoving, not really doing anything else. The third time I tried to walk away, she pulled my hair so hard that she managed to *rip* it from its roots and something inside of me snapped. I blacked out.

The next thing I remember is two teachers removing me from Joanne. I had broken her nose, jaw and her collarbone, and I was crying, saying, 'I don't want to fight. I don't want to fight. I don't want to fight.' This was so frightening; I was scared of who I'd become. I didn't want to be this person anymore. Luckily, I didn't get into trouble with the police because there were so many witnesses saying that I tried to walk away, and Joanne was attacking me. I told my parents I wanted to defer from school for a year and return to a school where nobody knew me; where I could become who I wanted to be.

My mum was mortified because they both came to this country to give us kids a better chance. Both my parents were pulled out of school so young. Mum was twelve when she was taken out of school to look after her siblings, and Dad started his electrician apprenticeship at thirteen. Neither of them were given the opportunity to have a good education, and here I was potentially giving all of that up.

Dad said I could defer for a year as long as I got a job that had potential. It took me two days to get a job as an assistant manager in a clothing store. Working in a family milkbar gave me loads of customer service experience, and I made a good impression on the manager. I had only been working for about eight months when the manager said I had to take leave because we were entering the peak season, and I couldn't have any time off for the next six months. I was so surprised to learn I was going to be paid while I took a two-week holiday, that blew my mind.

My parents had been on holiday to Perth with my brother and sister, and I couldn't go because I was working, so I decided to go to Perth. I became every mother's nightmare at seventeen and a half. I wanted to travel over 3,000km on my own. Once again, Dad said yes as long as I went and stayed at an aunt's place, only after I had pointed out that Mum was around seventeen when she got married and pregnant with a baby *(me)*, and all I wanted to do was go on a holiday.

My two-week holiday in Perth turned into six and a half years of travelling around the world. I might have been a YouTube sensation had YouTube been around then. I worked in hospitality, in retail, as an opal cutter, a jillaroo, on a prawn trawler and even as a governess/nanny. I worked many jobs and didn't care how hard it was; it gave me the income I needed to travel to my next destination.

I realised very quickly that people don't know who you're 'not', so you can be whoever you want to be. During my travels, I met the most extraordinary people, and I started to model the behaviours of people I liked and admired. I tried each behaviour on like a coat to see if it would fit me, and if it did, I made it my own. And if it didn't, I let it go. I learnt that you are more than your circumstances; I learnt that you can constantly reinvent yourself, and 'change' is a friend.

I am now a mother of seven glorious children, all created in another mother's womb, and I could not love them more if I had given birth to them myself. They taught me that unconditional love goes beyond genetics. In fact, genetics does not guarantee love, as both my parents have experienced as children, and so many others around the world have experienced. I am honoured and full of gratitude to have these now young adults as part of the very beautiful tapestry of my life.

THE BACKYARD PEACE PROJECT: VOL 1

Life is a journey filled with challenges, pain and disappointments. Every day, we encounter obstacles that test our resilience and push us to our limits. Yet, within each of us lies the potential to overcome these pain points, to live joyously and to find peace amidst the chaos.

I am driven by the profound understanding that while life is inherently challenging, those with a healthy mindset and emotional fitness can not only survive but thrive through adversity. I have witnessed firsthand the stark contrasts in how people respond to life's trials. What makes a mother, who has lost a child, sink into despair and neglect her surviving children, while another mother channels her grief into creating awareness and advocacy? What drives one person made redundant to spiral into addiction, while another seizes the opportunity to embark on a successful new career? How does one amputee push everyone away in rage and depression, while another becomes a Paralympian?

The difference lies in mindset and resilience. Those who thrive have discovered and cultivated their internal resources, enabling them to navigate life's storms with grace and strength. My passion is to guide others in finding these inner strengths, to help them develop the right mindset, and to support them in becoming the individuals they aspire to be.

I have an ambitious yet deeply personal mission: to help one million people live their truth and achieve their full potential. I want to create a ripple effect, where each person I help becomes a beacon of hope and strength for others. By fostering emotional intelligence and resilience, we can build a community of individuals who face life's challenges with courage and compassion.

Together, we can move away from unresourceful beliefs that cause pain and misunderstanding. We can create a world where everyone has the tools and support to thrive, regardless of the obstacles they face. This is my 'why' – my driving force and my dream.

Let's create a future where everyone can live their truth and be the person they were meant to be.

ABOUT LINDA

Linda Pierson is a mindset transformation coach with a bold heart and a sharp eye for potential. With over a decade of experience empowering individuals and teams, she helps people unlock emotional intelligence, reset unhelpful patterns and reclaim the life they actually want – not just the one they've settled for.

From coaching teens to mentoring burnt-out leaders, Linda brings a unique blend of warmth, strategy and real-world insight. Whether she is building leadership programs, guiding business owners to shift limiting beliefs or inspiring personal breakthroughs, she is here to remind people that creating the life you want is an inside job – and the tools to do it are within reach.

LINDAPTHRIVE@GMAIL.COM
linkedin.com/lindapiersoncoaching

MARIE ALESSI

A PIECE OF ME

Let me take you back to June 2018. I am spending all day texting and trying to call Rob – with no response. Only three days earlier we had walked with him to the station, as he was catching a train to the airport, off to another business trip to Perth.

We walked hand in hand, the boys on their bike and scooter – Happy Land. I snap a few photos, we hug, we kiss, the train leaves the station … and I snap another picture.

Two days later, we have a late-night phone conversation. We talk about Love and connection, as we often did. Rob shares, *'Babe, I met this young couple at the restaurant tonight, and they asked me to sit with them. I was so tired, but they insisted. I feel like I have left them with so much beauty to think about.'*

Rob promises to wake me at 7:30 the next morning. *'I love you!'*

'I love you too!'

I wake up at 7:31 the next day. Rob did not call. *'Bizarre,'* I think, send him a quick text and get on with my day. I drive Flyn to school; Jed's been up all night coughing, so he's staying home with me. I send Rob another text. A little while later I call …

'That's rather unusual,' I think, while my brain starts making a list of scenarios why he could've possibly not given me his wonderful wake-up call.

A smile crosses my face as I think of our wedding night, when he had lost his phone in the cab on our way to our cute little hotel …

I get busy looking after Jed, yet the unanswered texts and calls send me into a downward spiral, and I remember that Rob always leaves me his itinerary when he's away. So, I call the hotel.

'Hello, it's Marie Alessi. I understand my husband is staying with you. He was supposed to call me this morning, but I can't get hold of him. Could you kindly send somebody to his room to check on him?'

The moment those words leave me, I have a split second of a vision of Rob collapsing in the shower. I am physically shaking my head, telling myself to not allow my brain to go there, but I add, *'And can you please check in the shower?'*

I don't know what they must be thinking of me. I leave my number – nobody calls me back. I ring again; nobody answers the phone. Now I feel slightly paranoid, and I ring his boss. I explain the situation to James, and he promises to get back to me as soon as he would've spoken to his people in Perth.

Ten minutes later, my phone rings. James says, *'Marie, he hasn't showed up for his appointment this morning!'* The hopeful warrior in me collapses and drops her shield. I now know for sure that something has happened to him. Rob would never *not* show up – he is the most reliable person I know.

I call my best friend; she arrives within minutes, and we have a quick fact-chat; then she starts calling the first hospital in Perth. As I listen to her spelling our surname *'A–L–E– …'* my phone rings. A Perth number … My heart starts beating faster and I pick up.

'Hello, Marie speaking?'

'Is this Marie Alessi?'

'Yes!'

'Hello, this is Sergeant P from the coroner's office in Perth. Have you got somebody with you right now?'

'Yes, I do!' I respond in unbearable anticipation …

This is my *bilingual brain moment* of a lifetime. I had never heard the word 'coroners' before.

I learn fast as he continues, *'I am sorry to inform you that your husband deceased in a hotel room in Perth this morning.'*

I freefall into the SURREAL. I look at my friend and she hangs up the phone. *'Rob died,'* I say, completely numb.

REWIND to August 2015.

Rob called me on his way home from work. *'Babe, I'm gonna be about two hours late. There was an accident on Heathcote Road. There's a major detour around the national park!'*

Later, we learned that a young fire fighter, off duty, had died in a front-on collision with a truck. He left behind his wife and his sixteen-month-old daughter.

That night, on our bed, we had a conversation both raw and beautiful. It was based on a question that – unbeknownst to us then – would change the trajectory of our lives: *'What would you do if something was to happen to me?'*

FAST-FORWARD, back to Sergeant P's news in June 2018:

I am walking down the seven steps to our living room. My whole world moves in slow motion – as if the slowing down of time could reverse the news I had just received.

I am looking at my boys, busy with their iPads, waiting for me to make *'just another quick phone call'*, and I deliver the message you simply cannot sugarcoat.

We hug, we cry, and Flyn, our ten-year-old, asks, *'Who's gonna look after us now, Mum?'*

'I will; I will look after you!' I respond.

Jed, our second son, blurts out, *'I'm only eight and I'm not gonna have a daddy anymore!'* My heart shatters into a million pieces.

Then our promise that concluded our 'what if' conversation that night in August 2015 echoes in my heart: *'I want you to create the happiest life possible for you and the boys!'* I hear Rob say.

I had no idea how to do that, but this very promise became my North Star in our darkest hour.

The next day we flew to Perth to identify Rob's body. Some people questioned my decision to take the boys with me, but I knew I couldn't leave them behind. Their dad had just flown to Perth and didn't make it back home. The decision was instant. We were doing this together; all of it. The moment in the mortuary was indescribable, yet hugely important – and even more peaceful than expected – for all three of us.

We waited for the repatriation, organised a truly honouring Celebration of Life, and had Jed's First Holy Communion in the same week, only four days later.

That night I collapsed. I didn't see it coming. It started over some bickering between the boys, and after a few attempts of solving their disagreement, I called up to them, *'Boys, I just need peace and quiet!'*

It was like a valve had opened. I didn't realise how much I had been bottling up, and I couldn't stop myself. I started shouting that very sentence over and over, until I was screaming it from the top of my lungs: *'I just need peace and quiet!'*

I found myself on the kitchen floor, whacking the cupboard doors while primal screaming myself into an out-of-body experience. I cannot put into words how scared I was when my brain snapped back into functioning mode ... I had visions of the neighbours calling the cops or an ambulance on me; visions of me being carried away on a stretcher. *'The boys!'* One thought that jolted me back into my body. I was mortified.

What followed was a rather sobering conversation with my sons, trying to explain the unexplainable. It was in this conversation that I knew I needed to organise support for myself. I had arranged for Flyn and Jed to be able to see the school counsellor whenever they needed a space to retreat.

It was time for me to allow the same for myself. I worked with Emily for about four months. I couldn't believe the timing of her mum passing away shortly after we had our first session together. In a rather bizarre way, I felt we were sent to each other!

One day, sitting in her office, looking out to the ocean, I shared with her how overwhelming I found the load of expectations from society ... how we were supposed to grieve.

She looked at me ever so calmly and said, *'So, what does grief mean to you, Marie?'* I looked at her and said the first word that popped into my head, *'Empowerment!'* followed by, *'Wow, I did not expect that!'*

'I think I need to write a book about this,' I continued.

'I think you should!' Emily responded.

Five weeks later I published *Loving Life after Loss*. And when it ranked in the top one hundred bestseller list of Amazon Australia, I knew I had something the world needed.

With every decision, I learned to lean deeper into my inner guidance. I started seeing my path forward. I knew I wanted to continue what Rob and I had started together: A life full of Love and connection.

We had also planned to take the boys overseas and gift them a yearlong summer around the globe. I did not see it as possible to travel, grieve and homeschool them on my own for an entire year. And I would also not solo travel to South America with two young boys in tow.

Instead, I looked at what I can do – without Rob.

And only five months after Rob's sudden death, we boarded our trip of a lifetime, taking the boys away from all the first milestones to come without their dad: Christmas, New Years and both their birthdays ...

I knew we couldn't escape grief – that wasn't even my intention – but I knew there was a better environment to process the myriads of emotions that washed over us; far away from all the expectations that society places so heavily on you, simply unaware of how different your reality can be.

We even had the Santa and Tooth Fairy conversations in our private pool next to our overwater bungalow, overlooking the softest and most picturesque surroundings of the Maldives. I remember the sting in my heart, thinking, *'Not now, please give me one more year!'* – it felt like another little loss amidst their childhood.

We spent nine days with my godfather, an unexpected gift within our adversity, and rolled in black volcanic sand on the Canary Islands.

We spent Christmas with my mum in Vienna and New Years in Salzburg with my two closest friends, where we built a giant snow dragon with all our children. The boys climbed out of thermal pools surrounded by the majestic mountains south of Salzburg, to roll in fresh snow falling around us and jump back into the warm water. There was a lot of laughter, climbing up and sliding down two massive looping slides. A perfect way to celebrate Jed's ninth birthday.

During our six days in Paris, we walked to the Eiffel Tower at least five times and ate escargots! If anybody would have told me that I would eat snails, I would have vehemently dismissed it in disgust – yet Flyn played the 'dad card' on me … *'Wanna try some, Mum?'* He looked at me in anticipation.

'God, no!' escaped from my lips before I could think of anything more encouraging. His face dropped.

'Dad would've tried it with me!' he mumbled, barely audible. Well, that worked a treat – pardon the pun – because not only I, but even Jed, who is rather fussy when it comes to food, tried some. A truly memorable experience; it still makes us laugh when we chat about it!

I introduced my goddaughter to Flyn and Jed in Germany and redeemed a promise I had made to her almost thirty years prior: I took her out for ice cream – in winter – so much fun!

Jed lost a tooth at Universal Studios, where we celebrated Flyn's eleventh birthday, dancing with Alex the Lion, spending a day of lightness that we all needed. This was the final stop of our tour around the globe, before returning home to Australia to create our new normal.

The boys went back to school, into years six and four, and I picked up the pieces that had been waiting for me to come home.

It was about nine months into Rob's sudden death when I was doing something rather mundane in our bedroom, when I suddenly had what I now call a spiritual epiphany:

'This was our soul contract; Rob and I had chosen this journey on a soul level!'

It felt like somebody was sprinkling peace right into my heart, light as a pinch of cinnamon, settling ever so slowly into every cell of it, infusing me with a hint of warmth, acceptance and healing.

It was profound.

I felt my heart opening carefully, allowing the message in. I closed my eyes and pictured Rob and myself.

This sense of peace now washed all over me, hugging me so gently, with just the right amount of reassurance that I was able to handle at the time.

It took a few weeks of processing to fully understand the bandwidth of my realisation. It wasn't just a hidden gift in adversity; it was an intense connection with my husband beyond the realms, letting me know from the other side that we are okay; and I started to realise how powerful our soul contract was.

From this new sense of awareness, I noticed his presence more than ever. I felt his guidance in all my decisions. I started with breathwork shortly after, and it felt like finding a space between the realms where I could catch up with Rob.

In almost every session I would see him, sit with him and have what I would call 'non-verbal conversations'. Further, I started realising a few other soul contracts and, within them, deepest gratitude. It brought so much healing into some of my relationships – such as the one with my mum – and it felt like the initiation to my journey of becoming.

It took me a lot longer to start sharing about it; first with my closest circle, then bit by bit I spoke about it in various interviews – wherever it felt safe enough, as I understand that everyone holds different spiritual beliefs.

Yet, to me it felt like such a precious gift that I needed to keep to myself for a little while longer, until I fully grasped the essence of it.

It took me until today to wholeheartedly want to share it with the world in such detail. You, our valuable reader – and this very book – feel like the perfect container to be trusted with that piece of me.

Thank you!

ABOUT MARIE

Marie is a mother to two boys, a bestselling author, TEDx and keynote speaker and grief advocate. After her husband passed from a brain aneurysm, she chose happiness as their North Star. Little did she know that they had chosen this path for their young family years prior to Rob's sudden death. Rob had taught her the concept of two choices – and this path was followed in his honour; to continue the Love and connection they had.

Marie has become a shining example of choosing Love over fear and sadness. She offers hope, healing and happiness to the world, when people expect it the least and need it the most. In addition to her own books, Marie has been featured in countless media publications and has dedicated her life to bringing lightness into grief!

mariealessi.com

MELANIE RICHARDS
YOU ARE PURE LOVE AND HAPPINESS ...

For a long time, I thought love and happiness was something I had to chase. Something I'd eventually reach if I just worked hard enough, bought enough, was rich enough or found true love. But that belief – as innocent as it seemed – was the very thing keeping me unhappy. Because happiness isn't a destination. It's not something you find out there. It's something within you.

Growing up, I never really felt like I belonged. I was sensitive, quiet and felt and sensed deeply in a world that seemed to reward surface-level smiles, small talk and performance. I learnt quickly how to 'fit in', or at least, how to perform the part. I became a master at shutting down my heart, living in my head and being what I thought others wanted me to be; what I needed to be to be loved and accepted by everyone, including the society I lived in. But beneath the surface, I was sad. Disconnected. Lost. I didn't know who I truly was – only who I was supposed to be. I lived in my head, not my heart. My feelings overwhelmed me, so I pushed them down. I learnt to keep going, to just get on with it, and in the process, I abandoned the most important person in my life: my true self.

Looking back, I can see it clearly now. That sadness wasn't just depression – it was soul-deep disconnection. I wasn't broken. I was just far from home – the home inside my own heart and soul.

It wasn't just one thing that broke me open – it was a thousand moments. Becoming a mother was one of them. My children cracked me wide open in ways I couldn't have anticipated. They reflected to me all the love I wasn't giving myself. All the parts of me I had ignored. They challenged me to feel. To heal. To follow my heart. To live my soul purpose so that they could too.

There were also the quiet nights, the moments I thought, 'Is this it? Is this what life is supposed to feel like? There must be more?' And then in the silence … a quiet knowing from deep within: there is more than this. You are more than this.

My healing didn't happen all at once. It came in waves – sometimes gentle, sometimes tidal. I began spending time with myself. Not in isolation, but in intimacy. I started journalling, meditating and reconnecting with nature. I connected to my intuition and started to feel into the energy and the signs I received. I allowed myself to feel again – really feel. Not just the light, fluffy emotions but the grief, the anger and the fear. I dove deep into my feelings, my beliefs and into self-awareness of who I was beneath all the conditioning of who we are told we should be.

I stopped resisting. I stopped trying to 'fix' myself. And instead, I started loving myself – the real me; not the version I had created to be accepted. I realised I didn't need to become anything – I just needed to return to who I already was. And who I already was … was enough and was who I needed to be to have the more, the fulfilment, the love and the happiness I had always been searching for.

As I reconnected with myself, I began remembering things I had long buried. My sensitivity and special gifts were not a weakness or anything to hide; they were my superpowers. I was intuitive, telepathic and connected. I could feel and shift energy. I could sense what wasn't being said. I could feel spirit and communicate with souls –living and passed. I could heal things, and I just somehow knew how people could heal themselves. For years, I hid these gifts as I didn't want people to be scared. But I now understand: these are my gifts. And by living and using these gifts, I could finally be my true self, be fulfilled and be happy living my truth, my purpose. And most of all, these things that I have hidden can help to heal and guide others to their fulfilment, peace and true happiness.

From this point, everything changed. It changed within me in a way that changed my entire experience of life. I stopped chasing happiness and started embodying wholeness and embracing the true me; not my mind or body, but the spirit living within me. I stopped living from my head and started living from my heart – this is where the soul connection is with your body. I stopped resisting the pain, the problems and started allowing and learning from them instead. I let go of the fear, the worry. I let go of trying to be perfect and worked on knowing and accepting myself more.

And in doing so, I discovered something extraordinary: true happiness isn't about feeling great all the time, everything going great all the time, or having everything you want. It's about being whole and real. And wholeness only comes from embracing and loving all parts of you – even the ones you try to hide.

What I now know, with every part of my being, is this: You are pure love. You are divine energy in human form. You are a soul – wise, eternal, radiant – living in a human body, here to experience life, to learn, to feel, to grow, and to evolve. And everything that isn't love? It collapses in the face of love. When you stop believing every thought in your head … and start listening to the truth of your heart … everything shifts. It's not always an easy road, but it is certainly worth it.

What I've learnt, and now what I teach, is that the mind is limited. It creates fear, separation and judgement. But your soul? Your soul knows only love, only unity, only truth. When you live from your soul, life becomes magical – not because nothing bad ever happens, but because you are anchored into something unshakable. A knowing that you are always held, always guided, always enough. You are a miracle. You are love. And all the obstacles in the way, all the challenges and problems, are teaching you something. Teaching you more about yourself and your soul's path.

When you give yourself everything you've been seeking from others – attention, recognition, reassurance, love – you become free. You stop needing and you start overflowing, and when you overflow with love, you become magnetic. Let go and surrender to life, to the energy that is more intelligent than any human on earth. I want you to know this: it's safe to let go. It's safe to surrender. Everything will work out as it will anyway. You just need to connect back to your true nature, your soul and your soul's path.

You don't have to fight anymore; you don't have to strive. You don't have to earn your worth or prove your value, you are already enough. Let yourself be guided by love, by joy and by intuition. Love doesn't attach to anything. It allows it. It sees beauty in everything.

Say yes to life, all of it. The good, the painful, the uncertain. It's all here to wake you up, to return you to your truth. Even your darkest moments are gifts in disguise. They are not punishments; they are invitations. Opportunities to go deeper, to reconnect to your soul – the energy part of you that is eternal. Your light.

If there's one thing I want you to remember from my story, it's this:

You don't need to chase happiness, you need to remember who you are. You don't need to be perfect to be worthy. Feel what you feel. Honour your heart. Be honest with yourself. Love what is. You are not your trauma. You are not your past. You are not your fear. You can heal everything. They are all here to give you your purpose. You are love. You are light. You are a soul having a human experience, here to evolve, heal and make the world better just by being you and sharing your gifts with the world. So, find you, be you – bravely, unapologetically, kindly.

Loving and seeing beauty in everything is the path. Heal everything in its way. That is where the real magic begins.

So, bravely, I am choosing to live a soul-led life and doing what I truly love and where I am being guided to go; not by others, but by my intuition and my heart. This means being brave enough to stop hiding. To stop trying to fit in. To stop dulling my light to keep others comfortable.

I know I am here to inspire, to heal, and to guide.

I write books that speak to the hearts of children, teens and adults alike – because I want healing, inspiration and awakening to be more commonplace than the current fear we live in and are fed constantly.

I offer intuitive healing, coaching and energy readings – because I believe everyone has the capacity to heal whatever it is they may be going through or experiencing, and I want to assist others to heal and realise who they truly are, to live their full potential and purpose here.

I offer energy and intuitive healing, where I can use my gifts to heal and guide others. To clear and shift energy. To help bring the life force energy back and help reconnect people to their soul energy that they have often lost or shut down.

But most of all – I live from love. I live from truth. I live from my heart and soul. Fulfilment doesn't come from seeking happiness. It comes from being, and from living from this place of pure love.

ABOUT MELANIE

Melanie is an intuitive healing coach and energy healer, passionate about guiding others from suffering to peace and fulfilment. She helps people reconnect with their true essence and live in alignment with their soul's purpose. Melanie is already the author of several children's books that inspire young readers through gratitude, self-awareness and purpose.

melaniej.online

NATALIE LEDWELL

THE PRICE OF THE DREAM
FINDING PEACE IN THE CLIMB

People often meet me today and see the polished version of success: global impact, bestselling books, speaking tours and a thriving platform that has helped millions transform their lives. They see *Mind Movies* and the ripple effect it has had across the world. But what they don't see, what they couldn't possibly know just from the headlines, is the cost. The risk. The grind. The deep, quiet sacrifices that brought me here.

This journey, for me, has never been about overnight success. It's been a journey of deep soul excavation, of identity crisis, of fierce commitment to a vision bigger than me, even when it felt like that vision might break me.

And truthfully, it almost did.

THE DREAM THAT STARTED IT ALL

The seed of *Mind Movies* was planted when my then-husband, Glen, and I were running four different businesses in Sydney. We were living modestly, but we were dreamers, big dreamers. We believed in human potential. We believed that people were capable of extraordinary transformation, if only they were given the right tools.

A friend, whom we met through one of those businesses, came to us with the idea of creating video vision boards. We created a short digital video combining affirmations, visuals and music, a modern vision board with movement and emotion, and tested it on ourselves. The results were undeniable. We began sharing it with friends, then clients. The feedback was electric. We knew we were onto something.

But belief doesn't pay the bills. And dreams don't automatically find wings.

We poured everything we had into developing *Mind Movies* into a product we could take to the world. That meant late nights, endless editing, learning how to build a website from scratch and figuring out how to market something online with zero experience. We weren't digital marketers. We were passionate people with a big idea and no safety net.

Our first day launching a dinky little video on YouTube? Crickets.

We were devastated. Here we were, trying to bring something revolutionary to the world, and no one was buying. The next day, we had three sales. We were slowly on our way, very slowly on our way. But we were stubborn. Passionate. Perhaps slightly delusional. And deeply determined.

EVERYTHING ON THE LINE

By the time we decided to fly to the United States to attend a major internet marketing event, we were financially and emotionally exhausted. It was more like we had a big dream heading to the US, and that event, no money (just credit cards) but a big dream. We had no guarantees, no solid connections. But we knew that the US was the epicentre of online business, and if we could just get our foot in the door, we might still have a shot.

That seminar changed everything.

We met a mentor who believed in us. He saw the potential, helped us shape our messaging and connected us with some of the biggest names in the online personal development space. He didn't just open doors; he blew them off the hinges.

We worked incredibly hard, all while slowly accumulating over $100,000 in credit card debt. There was no plan B, no safety net. We were existing on a clear vision of what we wanted to create and the support of friends and mentors around us.

Our first major US launch brought in over $700,000.

Two years later, we'd hit $3 million in sales. It was a surreal pivot from barely scraping by to suddenly becoming one of the most talked-about success stories in the online transformational world.

From the outside, it looked like a fairytale. But internally, I was unravelling.

THE LONELINESS OF SUCCESS

When you're in the trenches building a dream, you don't always notice the fractures forming. The cracks in your health. The gaps in your relationships. The disconnection from your own joy.

Glen and I had always been a team. Building *Mind Movies* was a shared mission, and we were riding the wave together. But as we grew the business, the demands grew faster than we could keep up with. We were always working, always travelling, always performing.

The lines between our personal life and professional life blurred until they disappeared entirely.

We stopped communicating as partners and started operating as co-founders. Decisions were made quickly and sometimes defensively. We loved each other, but we were burning out. And neither of us knew how to say, 'I'm drowning.'

There were times I'd look in the mirror and barely recognise myself.

Yes, I was successful. But I was also tired. Anxious. Spiritually malnourished.

I was disconnected from my body. From my emotions. From my feminine essence.

I had become so good at driving, pushing, launching, scaling, solving …

I forgot how to *be*. How to receive. How to breathe.

THE TURNING POINT

There wasn't one dramatic moment that changed the course of our marriage. It was a series of quiet, gentle recognitions – those subtle shifts that accumulate over time.

The unspoken fatigue.

The evolving priorities.

The growing awareness that we were no longer walking in the same rhythm outside of our work.

We were still united in our purpose, still deeply respectful and supportive of each other, but our personal paths were beginning to diverge. And eventually, we both acknowledged – with care, love and compassion – that it was time for our relationship to evolve too.

Deciding to transition out of our marriage was not a failure. It was an act of grace.

Of honouring the truth of where we each were.

Of preserving the deep friendship, trust and legacy we had built together.

It was one of the most challenging moments of my life – and one of the most courageous.

I grieved. Not just the end of a chapter with someone I loved dearly, but also the version of myself I had been within that chapter. The Natalie who believed that peace would arrive after success. The Natalie who gave everything she had – heart, soul, time, energy – to the dream we were building.

I moved to Los Angeles on my own.

New city. New space. A fresh beginning.

And yes – it was scary.

For the first time in nearly two decades, I wasn't someone's wife.

I wasn't one half of a couple.

I was simply … me.

And in that space of quiet and uncertainty, I began to rediscover who that woman truly was.

Not through loss, but through reclamation.

REBUILDING FROM WITHIN

My healing didn't happen overnight. It took years.

Years of inner work.

Years of saying no to things that didn't feel aligned.

Years of saying yes to things that scared me.

Years of slowing down enough to hear my own voice again.

I started to feel into my body. I started dancing again. I started journalling not for content, but for clarity. I began working with spiritual teachers, diving into sacred feminine work and embracing all the parts of myself I had put on the shelf for the sake of being 'productive'.

And slowly, I came home to myself.

Peace, I discovered, is not a destination.

It's a practice.

It's the daily decision to honour your truth – even when it costs you.

Especially when it costs you.

I started operating from the new version of myself with intention. I made space for joy. I learned how to lead, embracing my softness. And eventually, love found me again – this time, a love rooted in mutual healing and deep presence.

THE TRUE CURRENCY OF SUCCESS

Looking back now, I wouldn't change any of it.

Not the failures.

Not the debt.

Not the heartbreak.

Because every part of that struggle forged in me a depth, a compassion and a resilience I didn't know I had.

I learned that peace isn't the *absence* of struggle.

It's the strength you build in the midst of it.

It's the clarity that comes when the noise dies down.

It's the freedom to choose differently next time.

Success, real success, is not just about what you build.

It's about *who you become* in the building.

It's about keeping your heart open in a world that constantly tells you to close it.

It's about creating from fullness, not from fear.

IF YOU'RE IN THE STRUGGLE …

To the woman reading this who feels like she's pouring her soul into something that isn't blooming yet, please don't give up.

But also, please don't abandon yourself in the name of the dream.

Your health matters.

Your relationships matter.

Your *peace* matters.

It is possible to succeed without self-destruction.

It is possible to rise without pushing everyone away.

It is possible to lead with both fire *and* grace.

And when you do, your life becomes the most powerful message you'll ever offer the world.

I stand here now not as someone who has it all figured out, but as someone who knows the cost – and knows it doesn't have to be that way.

May your struggle refine you.

May your peace guide you.

And may your dreams be built on the foundation of wholeness, not sacrifice.

Because the world doesn't just need your brilliance.

It needs your *being*.

And peace, real, grounded, radiant peace, is the most revolutionary act of all.

ABOUT NATALIE

Natalie Ledwell is a globally renowned personal development leader, speaker, and visionary entrepreneur, best known as the co-founder of **Mind Movies**, the revolutionary digital vision-board platform that has helped over ten million people worldwide manifest their dreams. Through her bestselling books, top-ranked *Inspiration Show* web series and international live events, Natalie has inspired audiences across over thirty countries to reprogram their minds, elevate their habits, and create extraordinary lives.

Passionate about harnessing technology for good, Natalie is also the founder of **Relieph**, an innovative app designed to guide users through trauma healing and emotional resilience practices. This latest venture reflects her lifelong mission: empowering people to break free from limitation, reconnect with their inner power and live from a place of joy and possibility.

Whether she's on stage, on screen or in the palm of your hand through her apps, Natalie Ledwell is a beacon of transformation. Her work continues to prove that when you combine intention with action, you can turn even life's greatest challenges into your most meaningful triumphs.

mindmovies.com
relieph.com

NICOLE PICCOLO
HOW DID I GET HERE?

How did I get here? How could I, the strong, hardworking, ambitious woman I thought I was – find myself in my forties, a single mum, with no money, living with my parents?

I kept asking myself what I had done to deserve this. And deep down, I blamed myself for the choices I had made, for not seeing the signs, for staying too long.

I've always been ambitious and worked hard for years to achieve big things. In my twenties, while working full-time in the financial services industry, I bought and sold several investment properties and made good profits. I purchased a house with no mortgage and invested in a franchise business with my then-partner. He ran the business while I continued to work my full-time job. But within a year, the business had failed, he had an affair, ran off interstate with the woman and left me behind to deal with the debts.

I was devastated. But I recovered from the separation and moved on – I managed to come out with significant savings.

Then I met someone new. He was a financial planner, smart and seemingly trustworthy. Things looked promising. Or so I thought.

The savings I brought into the relationship would help us build a future. We agreed to use the money to purchase a home in the future. Until then, he would invest it for me. Everything seemed to be working out fine.

But slowly, over the years, his behaviour began to change – not in obvious ways at first. He controlled the finances. For over ten years, we were together, and there were no joint accounts or discussions about managing money together. I didn't know how much he earned or where his money went. And if I asked, he'd either throw out vague numbers without proof, or I would be met with anger, accusations and silent treatment. So, I stopped asking. The part-time income I earned was enough for groceries, petrol and the kids' needs, while he 'took care of the rest'. I still had my savings that he had access to, but they were tied up in investments and were only to be used to purchase a house later.

On top of this, I endured emotional and mental abuse. He would get into angry moods and just go silent for days, sometimes weeks. There'd be no eye contact, no affection, just a cold, heavy presence. I never knew why. But I always blamed myself.

During these times, I'd be walking on eggshells, holding my breath until he'd finally go back to normal and speak to me again. Only then would I feel a moment of relief. But it never lasted long. Soon enough, something would trigger his anger, and the cycle would start all over again.

I dreamed of leaving, but the thought of only seeing my kids half the week terrified me. I couldn't imagine being away from them.

Then one day, everything unravelled. He confessed all my savings, that he was meant to be investing for our future, he'd gambled in high-risk investment products (products he knew I was against), without my knowledge. By the time he told me, it was all gone.

After years of hard work, I had nothing to my name. How could I have let this happen? Now, there was no way I could leave and support my kids on my own. So, I convinced myself to stay, just get through the day, then the next.

I felt trapped in this situation. I was ashamed. I had become someone who hid her personality, her goals, her light, anything that he didn't like that might trigger a reaction from him. I never told anyone. But looking back now, I realise that was one of my biggest mistakes.

The breaking point came when my daughter was just five, she was becoming more aware and was witnessing his behaviour. A couple of times, she commented about the way he was treating me. She was starting to see it and felt hurt by it.

That was it. I couldn't allow my children to grow up believing this was normal. I couldn't let my daughter think this is how women are treated. I couldn't let my son believe this is how you treat a partner.

For so long, I had convinced myself to stay for the kids, but now I realised I also had to leave FOR them.

I thought to myself: I chose now.

I started opening up to a couple of friends. When I told them, they were in shock.

He'd always come across as a great guy to everyone on the outside. No one could have imagined what he was really like behind closed doors. My friends encouraged me to start planning and to leave.

But it wasn't easy. There was fear, self-doubt and a lot of guilt. I worried I was breaking my family. I worried I wasn't strong enough. But I reminded myself: Staying in a situation that breaks you is not strength. Leaving to rebuild yourself is.

I eventually left, and for the first time in a long time, I was free. Not just physically, but emotionally. The weight had lifted. I wasn't walking on eggshells anymore. I wasn't afraid of how someone else would react to my words, my ideas or my happiness.

I had to start over from scratch, financially, emotionally and mentally. That's when the real work began, not just rebuilding my life but rediscovering me. But I felt stuck.

I hit rock bottom. I was depressed and felt immense guilt for my children, for my parents. I couldn't shake the feeling that I'd failed. I constantly questioned if leaving my relationship had been the right decision. My kids now had two homes. They went nights without me there to tuck them into bed. But deep down, I knew staying in that relationship would've caused even more harm.

One day, while talking to a friend about my situation, I broke down crying. She was surprised to see me that way, as I had always been the strong one. She referred me to a therapist friend of hers who runs a program to help people break free from emotional cycles.

That program became a turning point. During these sessions, I was able to shift my mindset and find peace in my situation. I learned to let go of how anyone had treated me in my past and not to blame anyone for where I was now. It was time for me to take back control of my life. I decided that I will no longer be attached to the past; instead I will attach myself to the future me. This is when I truly started to rebuild.

I delved deeply into self-help and personal development. I started with a gratitude journal. At first, it felt silly, but I stuck with it. Over time, I noticed how it shifted my focus. Each day, I found something new to appreciate.

The depression I was experiencing made sleep impossible. I started listening to positive affirmations while I drifted off. It was the only way I could rest my mind and fall asleep. And with all those positive 'I am' affirmations playing throughout the night, I slowly began to believe them.

Then I discovered the secret and the power of manifestation. I was skeptical at first, but learning the science behind it opened my mind.

I created a vision board and began doing guided visualisations. I stared at my vision board daily and felt myself as that woman. This changed everything. It opened something in me I didn't even know existed. My depression had lifted. For the first time in years, I felt a spark. I was seeing possibilities.

Through this journey, I realised my corporate job no longer aligned with my purpose. I wanted to do work that mattered. I set my sights on becoming a financial counsellor, particularly to support women affected by family violence – a cause close to my heart.

But the course I needed was expensive, and I didn't have the funds then. I learned about a scholarship for this course. The old me wouldn't have even applied – I'd have assumed I wasn't good enough. But the new me believed it was possible. I added it to my vision board and began to visualise myself receiving the scholarship and doing the course.

I tried hard with the application. I submitted it and tried to forget about it. Then one day, the email arrived: I got the scholarship!

Soon after, I applied for a role I really wanted, even though I lacked the experience and wasn't yet qualified. That old doubt crept in, but I caught it quickly. Soon after, I was offered an interview, but I was really nervous. Before each interview, I visualised myself being happy and successful in that role. So, each interview I had, I showed up as my future self.

After completing the final interview, I received a call. Not only did I get the job, but they also offered me a leadership role. Coincidence? Maybe. But I knew my mindset, my belief in myself and my visualisations had shifted something in me.

I dreamt about buying a home for me and my kids. I stuck to a strict budget and saved for months. The housing market was tough. Building prices had skyrocketed. I was limited in the amount I could borrow to purchase a house. Nothing seemed within reach. However, I continued to visualise a modern, spacious home for us.

A house and land package further out from the kids' school seemed my only option.

One day, I visited a land sales office. The sales rep told me there was no land left in my price range. I was crushed. But I knew not to give up and tried not to let those negative thoughts enter my mind. I didn't know what other options I had to buy my own home, so I went home and forgot about it.

A few days later, the sales rep called. One of his clients purchased a block of land a year ago, but his finance had just fallen through. And since the land was about to settle in a few weeks, the sales rep needed to find a buyer for the client before it settled. The sales rep also told me they will resell it at the original, much cheaper price from a year ago. Within my budget. I said yes immediately!

I paid the deposit and, in a few weeks, had settled on the land. My kids and I were so excited! It meant staying with my parents a bit longer, but we now had our own house to look forward to. And within eighteen months, we were finally in our brand-new home!

For many years after separating, I hadn't met the right man who fit into our lives. My kids were always my priority. So, I decided to stop looking for Mr Right and focus on us and our future.

But I still believed in love. So, I started to visualise my perfect partner – someone who aligned with our life and wouldn't disrupt it. I listed his qualities and

characteristics. I wasn't chasing, but I put it out there and trusted the universe. Not long after, I crossed paths with this man, and we started chatting. Over the following weeks, as we got to know each other, he started to tick off the boxes from my list. My perfect partner had come into my life unexpectedly and effortlessly.

Together, my new partner and I encouraged each other to dream big. He brought out that ambitious side of me. I loved my financial counselling work, but I always wanted to have my own business, where I had growth potential and more flexibility. I wanted more, but didn't know exactly what. So, I visualised new opportunities and success coming my way.

One hot summer's day in Melbourne, we'd been at the beach all day and decided to go out for dinner. Our favourite restaurants were booked out, so we ended up at a random pub. While waiting for a table, I noticed a shelf of second-hand books. One was by a woman whose wealth seminar I'd attended years ago. I took it home, curious to see what it was about.

In the book, she talked about her successful career as a life coach, and a light bulb went off. I hadn't thought about this before, but this was what I'd been looking for. It aligned perfectly with who I am and my work experience. I could take the tools I'd used to overcome my past and help other women like me, divorced, stuck and ready to build the life they deserve. I enrolled in a life coaching course and started my life coaching business, where I inspire abundance in others. Once again, I saw the universe work in my favour. That book was at that pub and I was meant to be there to find it.

My true purpose is to live an abundant life. This isn't about living in a mansion and driving a luxury car – it's about being abundant and fulfilled in all areas of life: family, friends, work, spirituality and relationships.

I work full-time and study. I love contributing to my community and increasing my social connections. I joined the school committee at both my kids' schools and volunteered at their sporting clubs.

Yes, life is busy, but I choose to be grateful for my full, abundant life.

And while I've been through hard times, I know many others have too. Helping others and giving back remind me to be grateful and send a ripple of goodness through my life.

I continue to visualise and show gratitude every day. I am continuously growing and evolving. Most importantly, I remind myself: my past does not define me. I made the choice to reset my life, and I found a way to do it.

The outcomes didn't have to be grand, glittering goals, just small steps. Each small step stretched my comfort one and belief in myself. After conquering each small step, more opportunities appeared. The best part? I was open to them. I was ready.

And I said yes.

The first step is believing. The next is persevering. It's so easy to slip back into old, negative mindsets. You have to keep going, even when it's hard, especially when it's hard. You have to believe that in the future, when you look back, it will all make sense.

Once you change your mindset, you have the power to step into your new Future – the version of you you've always imagined. That version has been quietly waiting inside you, hidden by pain, doubt or fear. Now is the time to let that person be free.

ABOUT NICOLE

Nicole is a finance and abundance life coach, who knows firsthand what it means to start from scratch and move forward with your life as a single mum after divorce. She now uses her story to uplift other women who have found themselves in that same place.

Having experienced challenges and breakthroughs herself, Nicole now shares the tools she used to create a life full of abundance with other women wanting to reclaim their power and step into the life they are meant to live.

Nicole had a successful career in the finance and investment industry for twenty years. After finding herself as a single mum, she felt this career no longer aligned with her life's purpose. She quit the corporate world and became a financial counsellor working with vulnerable people, taking a particular interest in women who have experienced family violence – as this is something she could directly relate to.

Nicole then started her own coaching practice, where she now helps women through their transformation. Through her coaching program, Inspired Abundance, Nicole shows her clients practical tools and mindset strategies she used to move forward and take back control of her life.

Nicole is driven by her passion to help women realise that an abundant life can be their reality. She will guide you, empower you, and walk alongside you as you step into the most powerful version of yourself, so you don't have to go it alone.

nicolepiccolo.com

PAUL BARNAT
FROM BURNOUT TO BREAKTHROUGH
TRANSFORMING ANXIETY INTO POWER

B reathing is key for living, without breathing we die! But breathing is not only that, it is much more. Breathing is healing, connection and empowerment. All this I found after a severe breakdown, which had to happen to make me see it clearly.

There was a time in my life when I looked like I had it all together on the outside, but inside, I was breaking apart. I was running a gym, managing staff and telling myself I was living the dream. The truth? I was burning out at a frightening pace.

I have been through anxiety bouts for most of my life, yet I had never experienced it this intense before.

Every day at work felt like walking into a pressure cooker. The owner micromanaged me so tightly that I couldn't breathe. He had cameras set up everywhere, so I never felt free to lead or make decisions. Even at home, I couldn't escape it. My mind would race at night, replaying the stress of the day and worrying about the problems I'd face tomorrow. Sleep rarely came … and when it did, it was helped along by alcohol.

I'd wake up with my stomach in knots, full of fear, dreading the alarm. On the outside, I told people I was okay. I even tried to convince myself I was proud of 'being a manager and running this gym'. But deep down, I knew I was falling apart. The anxiety, the sleeplessness, the drinking, the constant sense of dread, they were all signs. Signs I ignored until I couldn't anymore.

The breaking point came one morning when I simply couldn't go to work. My body refused. My wife had to call in sick for me because I couldn't even pick up the phone. I felt so anxious that I thought I was going to vomit. I remember sitting in my house, heavy with fear, sadness and anger, not knowing what to do. For the first time, I admitted to myself the truth: I wasn't okay.

The anxiety that I was experiencing was so severe that I became housebound for weeks.

That moment was painful … but it was also the turning point.

At first, I tried the obvious things: more sleep, meditation and listening to motivational talks. But nothing really stuck. My mind was too noisy, my body too restless and my nervous system was screaming at me (I was literally shaking). I needed something, anything to help shift this feeling.

The experience reminded me of all the personal development study and research I accumulated over the years; I had powerful tools to work on myself. One thing that really helped was getting outside. Walking by the beach, sitting on the rocks, I hid under a hood and sunglasses so that I didn't have to face people. Sometimes I cried. Sometimes I just stared at the ocean, letting the waves breathe for me. Nature didn't fix me overnight, but it began to open me.

Over time, I healed myself from the chronic condition using a handful of holistic lifestyle changes. Focusing on my breath and being in nature really helped me to reconnect to myself.

I took charge of my life and have not looked back.

Breathwork became the key piece of the puzzle. It wasn't just about 'relaxing'; it was about regulating my body, resetting my mind and creating space for clarity. Movement, nutrition, journalling and small mindset shifts started to follow. Piece by piece, I began to rebuild.

But the breakthrough didn't come all at once. I had setbacks. There were days when a phone call from the boss or a staff member would send me spiralling back into fear and anxiety. There were nights when depression crept in and I questioned everything – my work, my worth and even my future as a soon to be father.

And then came a moment I'll never forget.

Not that long ago, I was having a tough time in life trying to figure out my place in the craziness of the world in 2021, and I was sitting at a spot I would often go to sit on the rocks and meditate looking over the ocean.

This time was a little different … overwhelmed with so much sadness my heart was breaking, tears streaming down my face, I was in so much emotional pain. I closed my eyes and began to breathe deeply, to try and calm myself, although it was still hard to shake the sadness. I felt an urge to open my eyes and look behind me and there, wedged up in the rocks under a little waterfall, was a six-foot piece of bamboo all scratched up, looking rough and rugged as if it had had a tough time too.

It felt like a gift from nature.

I've suffered anxiety for as long as I can remember, and I remember that moment so clearly when I knew I had to do something about it.

Running, hiding, and medicating myself was not the answer. I was determined to face the fear and, even though I felt overwhelmed, the anxiety made me challenge myself to step through and do the things I feared.

I had been wanting to craft a didgeridoo for a long time. As I picked it up, I felt a wave of gratitude and a sense of purpose I hadn't felt in months. It was a time when I realised, I had drifted from my path into the opposite of what I really wanted to do in life.

Then remembering the amazing feeling I got from helping people to break through their challenges was the key to it all.

That rough, scarred bamboo became a symbol of my own journey;

beaten up, weathered, but still here, ready to be shaped into something meaningful.

That was my breakthrough, realising that breakdowns can become breakthroughs if we let them. Anxiety wasn't my enemy. It was a signal, a source of energy, even a superpower, when I learnt to work with it instead of against it.

Now, when anxiety rises before I coach a client or step onto a stage, I don't see it as weakness. I use it. It sharpens my focus, raises my awareness and fuels me to connect more deeply. My breath gives me the ability to transform fear into clarity, stress into strength, anxiety into action.

Today, I teach others the same tools; simple, powerful techniques that can be used anywhere, anytime. Because burnout and anxiety don't just disappear. They're part of being human. The difference is whether they control you, or you learn to work with them.

If you're reading this and you're in the middle of burnout, anxiety or overwhelm, I want you to know this: you are not helpless. You are not broken. And you don't have to do it alone.

Your breath is the first step back home to yourself. You've got this!

ABOUT PAUL

Paul Barnat is a dedicated coach and educator specialising in transforming anxiety into empowerment. As the founder of ReKnect, a coaching and training brand, he has developed the ReKnect Method, a unique blend of breathwork, movement and mindset training, to help individuals harness stress as a tool for growth.

Drawing from his own journey of overcoming burnout and anxiety, Paul discovered that breathwork was a missing piece of the puzzle for creating real-time physical and mental breakthroughs. He has since developed simple daily practices and frameworks that empower people to reconnect with themselves, align with their values, reclaim their time, and transform stress into inspired action.

With over twenty years of experience as a fitness and wellbeing coach, Paul has supported individual athletes and high performers in navigating the demands of growth, resilience and performance, both on and off the field.

As a global ambassador for the Backyard Peace Project, Paul is committed to spreading inner peace and fostering a global movement of mindfulness, emotional mastery and human connection. His mission is to equip individuals with the tools to transform their inner world, creating a ripple effect of peace, empowerment and positive change in their communities and beyond.

linktr.ee/Paul.focustheory

PHILIPPA SCOTT

FROM SILENCE TO STRENGTH
MY JOURNEY THROUGH BIRTH TRAUMA TO FANTASTIC FUTURES

THE MOMENT EVERYTHING CHANGED

I didn't know what birth trauma was. Not when I was drowning in it. Not even when I was crawling through the days that followed, wondering why the world felt like it had tilted off its axis, whilst everyone around me carried on as if nothing had happened.

What I did know was that something inside me had splintered the moment my first baby entered the world, and the world didn't seem to notice. I was surrounded by smiling nurses with their tick-box charts, congratulatory cards and people telling me how lucky I was to have a 'healthy baby'. I should be grateful! Meanwhile, I sat stunned, silenced and utterly torn apart in ways I couldn't even begin to articulate.

They told me everything went 'well'. The birth was 'successful'. Baby was 'perfect'. But no one, not a single soul, asked if *I* was okay. Not *really* okay. Not beyond the physical wounds that would eventually heal.

There are bruises that live in the body long after the skin has mended. Wounds that don't bleed but throb every time you look at your child and feel that knot of guilt for not experiencing what you were 'supposed to' feel. I loved my baby. Fiercely, completely, with every cell in my being. But that moment that was meant to be transcendent, empowering, transformative, had been hijacked by an external system that didn't hear me, see me or honour the woman I was beneath the patient gown.

The birth I'd planned, the experience I'd hoped for, the voice I'd tried to use, all of it had been swept aside by medical efficiency and institutional protocol. I came home not just with a baby, but with a silence so loud it filled every corner of my life. My instincts had been overridden. My voice was dismissed. My body was treated like a vessel rather than part of a whole human being with feelings, fears, and fundamental rights.

And in the place where empowerment should have lived, doubt took root and grew.

THE ART OF KEEPING BUSY

Like so many mothers before me, I coped the only way I knew how: I got spectacularly, exhaustingly busy.

I threw myself into motherhood like it was a performance that would be reviewed and rated. I ticked every box, read every book, baked the organic biscuits and attended every playgroup. I became the mother who volunteered for everything, organised community events, turned up early and stayed late, and never, ever said no to a request for help.

If I could just do it all, and do it brilliantly, then maybe I'd feel whole again. Maybe I could patch over the quiet ache that never left me, the sense that something fundamental had been stolen from me in that birthing room.

But busyness, I discovered, is a clever and seductive mask. It wears the face of competence whilst hiding deep, unspoken pain. It looks like success from the outside, whilst slowly hollowing you out from within.

And it wasn't just my family I poured myself into. I threw myself headfirst into the world of birth itself, as if I could somehow heal my own wounds by preventing others from experiencing the same.

PHILIPPA SCOTT

SACRED SERVICE AS SURVIVAL

I became a doula, one of those fierce, gentle women who sit beside labouring mothers, holding the space I never had. I witnessed the raw power of birth when it's honoured, the profound transformation when a woman is truly seen and supported. I ran women's circles, sacred gatherings where truth was spoken without shame, tears were honoured as holy water, and power was reclaimed one story at a time.

I helped build a birth centre. A place where women could give birth in dignity, with genuine choice, surrounded by reverence rather than routine. It was everything my soul longed for, to *be* the change I needed to see, to *create* what I didn't have access to when I needed it most.

And I had the chance to test everything I'd learned, everything I believed about birth, in the most personal way possible. I birthed three more babies.

The second birth was different; I had found my voice, even if it was still shaky. I knew my rights, I had my support team and I had doulas of my own. There was more power in that room, more choice. But still, beneath the surface, I carried the wounds from the first time. I was vigilant, protective and ready to fight for what I needed. It was better, so much better, but it wasn't yet peaceful.

The third birth brought even more empowerment. By then, I was deep in birthwork myself, surrounded by women who understood that birth is sacred, that a woman's experience matters as much as the baby's safe arrival. I felt held, honoured and seen. The healing was beginning, layer by layer. She let me shine!

The fourth birth, my last baby, I finally experienced what I'd been helping other women find all along. By then, I had done enough of my own healing work that I could truly surrender to the process. There was no fight left in me, no vigilance, no bracing for battle. Just deep, profound peace, a leaning into my intuition with a deep knowing. The birth I'd always imagined was possible, the one I'd been supporting for other women, became my own reality.

Each birth taught me something new about reclaiming power, about healing, about the way our bodies hold memory and our spirits hold truth. But it also showed me how much unfinished business I was still carrying, how the original wound kept colouring each new experience until I finally learned to tend to it properly.

For a time, this work, supporting other women, reclaiming birth for myself and others, felt like healing. The work was meaningful, transformative and essential. I was making a difference in the lives of women and families. I was part of something bigger than my own pain.

But what I didn't realise then, what took me years to understand, is that even the most sacred service can become another way of running. Running from the silence. Running from the unprocessed ache. Running from the parts of myself that still needed tending.

I gave and gave and gave until giving became my identity.

For ten years, I poured everything into that world, doula work, birth advocacy, women's circles, mentoring new birthworkers. I was always the one who had it sorted, the one others turned to when they were struggling. I was building something genuinely beautiful on the outside, creating real change, supporting countless families through their most vulnerable moments.

But inside, I was still running on empty. Still trying to fill the void left by my own unhealed trauma through the act of helping others.

PLOT TWIST: THE NEURODIVERGENT FAMILY

Then came the new chapter in our story that I never saw coming: neurodivergence.

One by one, my children began to show signs of being wired differently. Beautifully, uniquely, brilliantly, but also challengingly, in a world that wasn't built to accommodate their particular kind of magic. Suddenly, I was no longer just a mother trying to hold it all together. I was a translator, an advocate, a human shield, a detective trying to decode systems that seemed designed to exclude rather than include.

I spent my days navigating school bureaucracies, therapy appointments, support plans and educational meetings whilst still working full-time, still maintaining the facade of having it all sorted. The cognitive load was staggering, keeping track of different strategies for different children, advocating for accommodations, explaining and re-explaining their needs to people who often seemed determined not to understand.

But here's what I didn't anticipate: they were also growing up. My four little ones had become tween and teen girls, navigating the already complex world of adolescence with the added layers of neurodivergence. And just as I thought I could catch my breath from the diagnosis and intervention, they needed me emotionally more than ever before.

Four neurodivergent teen and tween girls under one roof, imagine the intensity, the brilliance, the sensitivity and the sheer emotional volume of it all. They needed a mother who could help them make sense of friendships that felt complicated, emotions that felt too big and bodies that were changing in ways that felt overwhelming. They needed someone who could hold space for their meltdowns about seemingly small things, who understood that their anxiety wasn't just teenage drama but genuine nervous system overwhelm.

With four different personalities, four different sets of triggers and four different ways of processing the world, the emotional labour was staggering. One might need deep water and silence, whilst another needed movement and music. One would shut down completely, whilst another would explode with feeling. They needed me to be calm, present and regulated, to be their emotional anchor in a world that often felt chaotic and unpredictable. They needed a nervous system that could co-regulate with theirs when they were overwhelmed, someone who could help them navigate the social complexities of being different in a world that prized conformity.

But my own nervous system was stretched to breaking point, still carrying the unresolved trauma from years past, now layered with the constant stress of advocacy and the grief of watching your children struggle in a world that doesn't get them. How could I be their safe harbour when I was drowning myself?

And finally, after sixteen years of pushing, proving and performing, my body said enough.

THE RECKONING

It wasn't just burnout this time. It was complete systemic collapse.

I remember lying on the couch one morning, unable to lift my head without the room spinning. My limbs felt like they were filled with concrete. My thoughts scattered like leaves in the wind. It felt like grief and rage and complete depletion all rolled into one overwhelming wave of *I cannot do this anymore.*

The world had a clinical name for it: adrenal fatigue. But for me, it was a reckoning. My nervous system had been waving red flags for years, and I had dismissed every single one as weakness, as something that a stronger woman could push through with enough green smoothies and positive thinking.

But I wasn't weak. I was *wounded*. And the wound wasn't just in my exhausted body, it was in my story. In the unspoken pain of that first birth, a childhood and adolescence filled with expectation. In the years of silence that followed. In the bone-deep belief that I had to earn my worth through endless doing and giving and being everything to everyone.

I was ready now, not just to cope or manage or survive, but to actually heal.

But I didn't know what I was looking for. I just knew that something needed to fundamentally change, not just how I managed my days, but how I existed in my own body, in my own life. I didn't even know how to search for what I needed, or what words to use to describe the kind of help that might actually work.

In my desperate search for a path forward, I bravely leaned in with curiosity and discovered The Richards Trauma Process (TRTP). It felt like a homecoming, a process that addressed not just the obvious wounds but the deep-seated patterns of perfectionism, people-pleasing and the belief that love had to be earned, all woven into my nervous system long before my first birth. By working directly with my subconscious mind and nervous system, TRTP allowed me to release trauma without the need to extensively relive past pain. This journey shifted my reality beyond all recognition, finally bringing the parts of me that had been frozen in fight, flight or freeze for sixteen years into a new-found and profound safety.

THE TRANSFORMATION

It didn't just change how I felt, it changed who I believed myself to be at the most fundamental level.

I stopped seeing myself as broken, as someone who needed to be fixed or managed or carefully maintained. I stopped seeing my coping strategies as character flaws and began to recognise the incredible strength it had taken to survive and the profound courage it now took to stop merely surviving and start actually living.

For the first time in years, I could feel my own feelings without being overwhelmed by them. I could be present with my children's big emotions without being hijacked by my own nervous system. The constant background hum of anxiety that I'd assumed was just part of my personality began to quiet.

I started sleeping through the night. My energy returned, not the manic, driven energy of survival mode, but a sustainable, grounded vitality. I found myself laughing more, crying when I needed to, instead of holding it all in, making decisions from a place of clarity rather than reactivity.

And when the dust settled, something entirely new began to bloom: Fantastic Futures.

THE DEEP WORK OF HEALING

Through my work with parents, I gently hold space for the wounds that run the show behind the scenes. We don't just talk about parenting strategies or behaviour management techniques. We talk about the mother's story, the birth that didn't go as planned, the childhood that left marks and the relationship patterns that keep repeating. We explore the father's fears of failing, of becoming like his own father, of not being enough.

We bring the unspoken into the light where it can be met with truth and compassion. And through TRTP, we release it, not temporarily, but for good.

When trauma softens its grip, everything changes. The voice in your head becomes kinder. Your home feels less like a battlefield and more like a sanctuary. Your children respond differently because you show up differently, not because you're trying harder, but because you're no longer operating from a place of threat.

THE TRUTH THAT CHANGES EVERYTHING

This is the essence of what I've learned through my own journey and through walking alongside hundreds of other parents: we parent from our nervous system, not from our intentions.

That one truth changed everything for me and continues to transform the families I work with.

You can have all the parenting knowledge in the world. You can read every conscious parenting book, attend every workshop and follow every expert on social media. But when your nervous system is stuck in survival mode, when it's still bracing for the next blow or running from an old wound, your body will override your best intentions every single time.

Because trauma isn't really about what happened to us. It's about what got *stuck* inside us.

It's the incomplete stress responses trapped in the body, the fight, flight, freeze reactions that never got to complete their natural cycle. It's the moments where we felt powerless, unseen, unsafe and never got to finish the story. So those parts of us stay frozen in time, waiting for a resolution that never came.

This is why trauma can be so quiet and invisible. It doesn't always look like PTSD or dramatic flashbacks. Sometimes it looks like overworking, people-pleasing, perfectionism or emotional shutdown. Sometimes it's rage that feels bigger than the moment, or shame that clings to your every move as a parent.

For sixteen years, I was functioning, busy, capable and even inspiring to others. But my nervous system was stuck in high alert, and my body was paying the price, whilst my family lived with the ripple effects of my unhealed pain.

THE GENTLE REVOLUTION

The turning point was understanding that healing doesn't have to be long, hard or re-traumatising. I didn't have to retell every painful story or explain every detail of what went wrong. I simply had to help my body understand that it was safe now. That the threat was over. That I could finally, truly relax.

When this happens, when trauma is cleared at the nervous system level, people often report that things which used to feel like mountains suddenly feel manageable. They respond instead of react. They feel more present in their bodies, more able to connect, freer to enjoy life again.

For parents, the ripple effects are profound and beautiful. You stop feeling hijacked by your child's meltdowns. You don't spiral into guilt every time you raise your voice. You find your *choice* again because your nervous system is no longer calling the shots from a place of perceived threat.

And perhaps most importantly, you stop passing on what was never yours to carry in the first place.

THE INVITATION

If you're here, reading this, and you're tired, soul-deep, bone-weary tired, I want you to know that you're not alone. If you're wondering why all the tools and strategies haven't worked, why you can't seem to 'stay calm' despite your best efforts, why you keep repeating patterns you swore you'd never repeat, please hear this: It's not because you're a bad parent. It's not because you're lazy or broken or fundamentally flawed. It's because your system is still in survival mode, and survival can't make space for the softness and connection you long for. But healing is possible. There are gentle, effective ways to complete trauma, not by talking about it endlessly, but by allowing your nervous system to shift into safety.

No matter how long it's been. No matter how deeply buried it feels. No matter what you've tried before that didn't work.

You are not too far gone. You are not beyond help. You are simply waiting to return to the safety that is your birthright. And when you do, everything changes, not just for you, but for the generations that follow.

The silence can end. The strength is already within you. And the future you're creating for yourself and your children, truly, can be fantastic.

ABOUT PHILIPPA

Philippa Scott is a transformative therapeutic birth and parenting coach with a powerful mission to heal generational patterns and empower families. With over two decades of experience, she specialises in helping parents break through emotional barriers and create profound family transformations.

Through her unique approach at Fantastic Futures, Philippa uses advanced therapeutic techniques to guide parents beyond traditional coaching. Her work focuses on healing deep-seated emotional wounds, understanding intergenerational trauma and creating sustainable positive change in family dynamics.

As a seasoned coach and mentor, Philippa doesn't just offer advice – she provides a revolutionary pathway for parents to rewrite their family's emotional narrative. Her expertise lies in helping individuals recognise and transform unconscious patterns that impact parenting and personal growth.

Drawing from her own journey of healing and resilience, Philippa brings authenticity and deep compassion to her practice. Her approach combines psychological insights, therapeutic interventions and practical strategies to support parents in creating healthier, more connected family experiences.

THE BACKYARD PEACE PROJECT: VOL 1

Philippa's mission extends beyond individual healing; she's committed to breaking cycles of emotional limitation and empowering parents to create lasting, positive change for themselves and future generations.

bio.site/fantasticfutures
fantasticfuture.com.au
philippascott.com
instagram.com/fantasticfuturesbirth_beyond
facebook.com/fantasticfuturesaustralia
rss.com/podcasts/the-family-architect-parenting-by-design-rather-than-by-default

SANDY FORSTER

THE MAGIC OF MONEY, MINDSET AND MANIFESTING MILLIONS

Back in the good old days (not), my life was a constant financial struggle. I was a divorced mum raising a baby and toddler on my own, $100,000 in debt and trying to survive on a single-parent welfare payment of around $15,000 a year. I was working seven days a week in a swimwear business that no longer brought me joy or a profit, and I felt like I was getting nowhere. Money was a constant source of stress; it consumed my thoughts, it scared me and no matter what I did, it always felt out of reach.

There were so many tough moments in my journey, but one that really hit me hard was having to walk through the dream home I'd built with the money from my divorce, combined with a loan. Wandering room by room, saying goodbye because I couldn't afford to keep it any longer broke my heart. I remember crying and feeling like I wasn't just losing a house, I was saying goodbye to my dreams.

Before I discovered the power of manifestation and personal development, my mindset was stuck in scarcity. I honestly believed wealth was for 'other people'. I thought work was just a way to pay the bills, not something you could actually love. I had all the usual limiting beliefs: 'money doesn't grow on trees', 'you need money to make money', 'rich people must be doing something shady'. Deep down, I felt powerless, hopeless and worthless when it came to money. I was constantly asking myself, 'What's wrong with me?'

My financial situation impacted my entire life, including my self-worth. When I couldn't afford even basic things for my kids, like a new shoes before my daughter's school dance or an ice cream cone when we were at the shops, I felt I was failing as a mum. It squashed my confidence and self-worth and made me feel short-tempered and ashamed. I knew I was a good person, but I couldn't figure out why my life was such a mess. The stress around money created guilt, shame, fear and a constant feeling of not being good enough or capable enough to ever get ahead.

One of the biggest shifts was understanding that it's not just about what you do, it's about how you *think and feel* while you're doing it. I had to move from constantly focusing on lack to deliberately focusing on even the tiniest signs of abundance. I also had to let go of the belief that money was hard to earn or that wanting more of it was somehow selfish. I started embracing the idea that abundance was available to everyone, even me, and the more I have, the more I can give, the bigger difference I can make in the world.

I had to completely rewire the limiting beliefs I'd grown up with and let go of the guilt I felt around simply *wanting more*. I had to stop believing I needed to become someone totally different to be successful. For a long time, I felt like a fraud, like I didn't deserve to be wealthy because I'd dropped out of high school or made so many stupid financial mistakes. But the biggest block of all? Feeling like I wasn't good enough because I wasn't organised, polished or what I thought a 'real' businesswoman should be. Once I finally began to believe that I was *worthy* of abundance and I could be successful exactly as I am, everything started to shift.

Little by little, my life transformed and I went from welfare to millionaire. Not because I had a perfect plan, but because I was willing to shift my mindset, take inspired action and keep going even when it felt impossible. I went from being a single mum, $100,000 in debt on welfare, to a millionaire. Because I discovered the power of the mind, got obsessed with personal development, and step by step, I turned my entire life around. I looked around at other women and thought, 'If I can do it, so can you.'

I felt I knew a secret that could change everything for them and decided to create a community where women could support each other while learning how to attract prosperity from the inside out. My vision was to combine spiritual principles with practical strategies, and empower women to believe in themselves, attract abundance, and create a life they truly loved.

All the programs and courses I've created since then were born from a combination of desperation and inspiration. After discovering and mastering manifesting and transforming my life using the law of attraction, mindset work and personal development, I was making more money than ever before. I wanted to share my tips and secrets with the world.

Today, my website wildlywealthy.com and my Wildly Wealthy Women podcast are all about empowering women – spiritually, emotionally, energetically and financially. It's about helping women realise they are the creators of their own reality, and that they absolutely can live a life of abundance, freedom and joy. Through all the things I love and teach – mindset, manifesting and simple yet powerful processes – I help women unlock their potential, dissolve their money blocks and create wealth from the inside out. It's not just about the money, it's about becoming the version of yourself who can manifest it, handle it, enjoy it and use it to make a difference.

I think there's a huge limiting belief women often have that either money is not for them or that they have to sacrifice everything to get it. So many women carry guilt around wanting more, or they think they have to hustle twenty-four seven to succeed. But abundance doesn't have to come through struggle. I truly believe the biggest shift is realising you don't have to choose between success and freedom, or between money and meaning. You can have both. You can create a wildly wealthy life doing what you love, in a way that feels good and aligns with your values

Everything I now teach is based on rewiring your mindset and shifting your energy first. I blend metaphysical tools like visualisations, affirmations and the law of attraction with grounded practical steps, so women can align their thoughts, feelings and actions with the abundance they want to create. I also incorporate cutting-edge neuroscience, because science now confirms what spiritual teachers have been saying for centuries – your brain literally rewires itself based on what you focus on, feel and repeat consistently.

As well as my money mindset courses, I also train women around the world to be internationally certified coaches using all the manifesting, neuroscience and law of attraction principles I teach. In everything I do, I guide women to create new neural pathways that support prosperity, worthiness, and possibility. I give them the structure, support and inspiration to stay consistent, embody a new identity and take inspired action. That's when the magic happens, not from forcing or pushing, but from becoming the version of yourself who naturally attracts success.

But believe me, it hasn't always been easy. I've had my fair share of criticism and major challenges! Early on, there were people who thought I was 'too out there' talking about energy and the law of attraction – in fact, I did too, and that held me back a lot. People didn't take me seriously because I spoke about money in a way that blended the spiritual with the practical, which was not really done at the time.

I've also faced my own internal challenges, especially around how my brain works. Let's just say I don't always think or operate the way others do, which makes certain things harder behind the scenes. Staying focused, being structured or following the traditional success path has never been easy for me. But I've come to realise those differences are also part of my magic. The truth is, I'm just me, someone who loves the colour pink and embraces the 'woo-woo'. I know I'm not everyone's cup of tea, but by showing up as my real, excitable, passionate self, I attract the women who are aligned with my message, ready to think differently and take action to manifest the life of their dreams.

But there were definitely moments I felt like a fraud, especially during times when I was still working through my own money stuff – which let me tell you is a life-long process! Even though I've made tens of millions of dollars, I've had times where things weren't flowing and I questioned whether I was really cut out for this. The pressure of being a mentor while still growing myself makes me want to hide sometimes. And the challenges of creating an online business for me were enormous, as I am not techie and get overwhelmed with 'all the things', and I've spent many hours crying and wanting to go and live on a desert island and give it all up. But deep down, once I started, I knew this was my purpose. I just remind myself that I don't have to be perfect to help others, I just have to be willing to keep showing up and doing what I love.

And to be honest, the thing that pulls me through in those crappy moments is the women in my community and hearing success stories from people I've never met. Seeing them have breakthroughs and transformations reminds me why I created my business in the first place.

Like Denise D T from Australia, who read my book, joined my coach training academy, then did my author course … first she manifested a trip around the world fully paid, and now has a multimillion-dollar online business and has written three books.

Or Linda for the US, who got a letter out of the blue saying her loan of $95,703 was wiped off, she didn't need to pay it back.

And even the person who sent me a message by Instagram saying they didn't see a way out of their terrible financial situation and were so desperate they were going to commit suicide, but somehow got my book, read it, put things into place and things totally turned around. They manifested money, paid off their debt and had now started a business.

I have thousands of stories like that, and they still give me goose bumps when I read them, so even when things are not going to plan for me – because life is life, and it gets like that sometimes – I know I'm making a difference, and it inspires me to keep going.

That, and my own commitment to growth and actually practicing the processes I teach. I love to dive into a visualisation, do some affirmations or go back to my 'why'. I connect with the vision I have for my life and the impact I want to make. That always gives me a kick up the butt and keeps me moving forward.

When it comes to practices that inspire me now, I try and mix it up, but I have some that I love to do daily … meditation, walking by the ocean, visualisations and diving into inspiring books, podcasts or courses are my 'go-tos'. I also find I stay super inspired by actually teaching others. Every time I coach, speak or create something new, it reminds me of the power we all have to transform our lives. And a biggie … gratitude. No matter what's going on, I'm always coming back to what I'm grateful for. That simple practice can change everything.

And although my message is about manifesting and money, I believe being wildly wealthy is about so much more than money. To me, it means having the freedom to live life on your own terms. It's about waking up every day feeling excited and inspired, knowing I'm making a real difference in people's lives, whether that's donating to a cause I'm passionate about or transforming someone's life through my courses or podcast, that's what makes me feel truly abundant. It's not just about the money (although keep that coming, thank you very much!), it's about having choices and that blissful feeling of freedom – which, if you haven't already guessed, is my number-one value!

I feel extremely blessed that I am doing what I love, and it's also my income. It took a while to get here, but I think that makes the success so much sweeter. If I had the chance to go back and speak to my younger self, I'd say: 'You are more powerful than you know. Money is energy, and when you align with it, it will flow. You don't need to have it all figured out. Even if you have no idea what your purpose is right now, trust that it will reveal itself, and when it does, it will be more fun, fulfilling and full of gratitude than you can imagine. Just keep dreaming big, take one step at a time and know deep down that you are absolutely worthy of everything your heart desires.'

And if I could slip in a little PS to my younger self, it would be, 'Buy $1,000 worth of something called Bitcoin in 2009 … You won't regret it.' Haha!

For all the women who have been impacted by my teachings, I'd love them to remember me as 'Sandy from the Sunshine Coast' who helped remind them of their magic, helped them shift their mindset and showed them that anything is possible when you align your thoughts, feelings and actions. I hope they remember me as someone who's just like them. Not some guru, just someone who turned things around and loves to share what worked. Just a friend who cheered them on, believed in them when they forgot to believe in themselves, and most of all, showed them how to create more freedom and abundance in their life than they ever dreamed possible.

And my final message to anyone reading this, no matter where you're starting from, whether you're drowning in debt, stuck in a job you hate, quietly craving more, doing great but want to take it to the next level or just want to do something different you can absolutely change your life. I went from welfare to millionaire not because I had special skills or the perfect plan, but because I was ready, willing and able to change the way I thought, and I kept going even when it was hard, even when I couldn't see any results. So please don't give up on your dreams. Start where you are, find a mentor you resonate with, become empowered, believe in possibilities and take inspired action. You truly can create a life that is filled with prosperity, fun and freedom. If I can do it, you can too!

ABOUT SANDY

Sandy Forster is a money mindset mentor for women worldwide who are ready to experience more prosperity and freedom in their lives.

She's climbed to the highest camp on Mt Kilimanjaro, meditated in complete silence for ten days, watched the wildebeest migrate across the Serengeti, trekked the Inca Trail to Machu Picchu, dived with dolphins in Hawaii, wandered markets with Moroccan nomads in the High Atlas, white water rafted down the Zambezi and was helicoptered off Mt Everest where she almost died trekking to Basecamp.

She's swum in Sacred Mayan underground caves, flown by helicopter over Victoria Falls, danced with Masai tribesmen in Kenya, travelled to over fifty-two countries, gone from welfare to millionaire, written a bestselling book, won multiple business awards, is host of the popular podcast *Wildly Wealthy Women* and been personally invited by Jack Canfield to be a member of the world's most awesome group of transformational leaders, experts and authors on the planet!

Sandy loves showing women that anything is possible, and then empowering them to break through their blocks, manifest more money, and create a life they're truly passionate about. She's the founder of the Inspired Spirit Coaching Academy and has personally trained over 1,500 women around the world to be internationally certified coaches.

She lives in her own tropical paradise near the beach in sunny Australia and is visited by wild kangaroos grazing on her acreage every afternoon.

Get your free meditations and abundance affirmations: wildlywealthy.com/bonus

wildlywealthy.com

Discover how to become an internationally certified coach: inspiredspiritcoachingacademy.com

SANDRA SPADANUDA

THE GIFT OF HOLDING SPACE
WHAT YOUTH WORK TAUGHT ME ABOUT PEACE

I used to think peace meant stillness – something you found in quiet mornings or meditative breaths. But then I found myself sitting cross-legged on a red dust-covered youth centre floor beside a teenager who hadn't spoken in days, his silence louder than any words. There were no solutions I could offer. No tidy ending. Just presence. Just breath. Just the slow, human act of being there. That was the moment I first understood – peace isn't always gentle or polished. Sometimes, it's showing up in the mess. Sometimes, it's listening without trying to fix. Sometimes, it's holding space for someone else's storm, and in doing so, learning to weather your own.

Youth work is rarely still. It pulses with motion, emotion and moments that can crack you open without warning. It happens in cars, in courtrooms, in hospital waiting rooms, at kitchen tables, and at youth centres. Sometimes, it's laughter echoing through a campfire circle. Other times, it's the heavy silence that follows bad news.

Over the last twenty-seven years, I've worked across the not-for-profit, government and business sectors within the youth, community and social services fields. I've held roles that required reports, policies and high-level planning – and others that simply required me to sit beside a young person who had no one else. And through it all, one truth has remained constant: the work is never really about you. It's about presence. Connection. The sacred space between two people when one says, 'I don't know what to do,' and the other replies, 'You don't have to do it alone.'

Holding space, I've learnt, isn't a skill you can list on a résumé. It's a practice. A discipline. An act of radical stillness in a world that tells us to fix, solve, and move on. To hold space is to resist the urge to offer answers. It's sitting in discomfort, allowing stories to be told or not told. It's witnessing someone in their pain without trying to tidy it up or turn it into a teachable moment. And, often, it's where real healing begins.

People often ask me what youth work is really like. They imagine recreation programs, school talks and maybe the occasional crisis intervention. But they rarely see the heart of it: the whispered confessions shared on long drives, the slow trust built over months, the last-minute house moves to keep a young person safe. They don't see the cumulative emotional weight we carry or the deep wells of love we draw from again and again – not because we're heroes, but because we've seen what happens when no one shows up.

And yet, amidst all this chaos, I've come to realise, is where peace lives. Not the Instagram-worthy kind of peace with candles and clean lines, but the messy, lived-in kind. The kind that comes from knowing you're in the right place at the right time, doing something that matters, even if no one else sees it. The kind that sits quietly in your chest at the end of a long day, reminding you that connection is the most powerful force on earth.

I didn't become a youth worker to find peace. But I found it anyway – in the faces of the young people I've walked beside, in the families I've supported, and in the spaces we've created together where healing could begin, even if only for a moment.

If you stay in this work long enough, the young people become your greatest teachers.

There was a boy I'll call Mason – barely thirteen, yet already hardened by things no child should witness. He barely spoke when we first met.

His file said 'aggressive', 'defiant' and 'oppositional'. But I've learnt over time that those words are often just armour. What they mean is hurt. Unheard. Unprotected.

We started meeting at a park. No pressure. Just two people sharing silence. After weeks of small nods and shrugged answers, he finally looked me in the eye one day and said, 'You're not like the others. You wait.' And I did. Not because I knew what to say, but because I knew how it felt to have no one wait for you.

There was no grand breakthrough that day, no Hollywood moment. But he came back the next week. And the week after that. Over time, Mason showed me that peace isn't always about fixing the chaos. Sometimes, it's simply the absence of judgement. It's making space for someone to exhale, to be seen without being labelled. That kind of peace changes people. It changed me.

Then there was Aaliyah; a bright, fierce girl with fire in her eyes and grief stitched into her every sentence. Her mum had passed unexpectedly, and she'd been passed from placement to placement like a problem no one knew how to solve. We connected at an on-country camp I was running – a space designed for young women to reconnect with themselves and each other. One night, sitting beneath a sky full of stars, she asked me, 'Do you think people can still grow up good, even if the world gives them the worst?' My throat tightened. I didn't offer clichés or platitudes. I just said, 'Yes. Because you're already doing it.'

She leaned into my shoulder and didn't say another word. That moment wasn't just for her. It was for me, too. A reminder that peace isn't always quiet – it's sometimes a soft shoulder and a hard truth shared under the stars.

So many others come to mind. A boy who drew his trauma in vivid colours because he couldn't find words. A young mum who let me hold her baby while she cried for the life she wished she'd had. A teen who asked if she could call me 'Aunty' because she didn't know who else to trust.

I've watched young people fight their way back from despair, from addiction, from years of systems failing them. And somehow, they still show up – with jokes, with dreams, with a hunger to be held in hope. It's humbling. It's gut-wrenching. It's beautiful. And it taught me that peace is less about perfection and more about presence. Not about answers, but attention. Not about avoiding pain, but being willing to sit beside it.

People think this work is about saving others. But truthfully, it's saved me more times than I can count.

It has reminded me, again and again, that no matter how heavy the world feels, connection is a lifeline. That holding space for someone else doesn't drain you – it deepens you. And that peace, real peace, is found not in isolation, but in community. In showing up for each other. In the moments when nothing needs to be fixed, only felt.

The more I leaned into the art of holding space, the more I noticed its ripple effect. What started in one-on-one conversations with young people became a quiet framework for how I moved through the world. It changed how I led teams, how I built programs, how I showed up as a foster carer, a community advocate, and a woman navigating systems often stretched beyond their limits.

In youth work, we're often taught to focus on goals – recording our contacts, risk assessments, behaviour plans and timelines. Those have their place, but what I found to be just as powerful was something far less tangible: the feeling a young person gets when they walk into a room and feel safe. When they're not judged by the notes on their file, or their last mistake, or their postcode. When they're met with dignity, not pity.

That feeling – that's peace in practice.

It's what led me to co-found Blue Beanie Projects, a grassroots charity focused on child and youth mental health and resilience building in regional and remote communities. We began in honour of a young life lost, but we continue in honour of every young person still here, still fighting, still hoping. Our programs aren't designed to 'fix' young people. They're designed to hold them. Celebrate them. Remind them that their story matters.

Through Blue Beanie, I've witnessed healing unfold in unexpected ways. I've seen young people light up when they walk a runway for the first time; not because it's about fashion, but because someone believed they were worthy of being seen. I've seen tough conversations held with softness. I've seen entire communities come together around creativity, culture, and connection. And through it all, I've seen how powerful it is when we choose to lead with heart.

That choice – the one to lead with heart – is also what fuels Pilbara Shine, one of our signature creative youth projects. Through styling workshops, photo shoots and fashion shows, we give young people the tools to express who they are, not just what they've been through. We let them write their own narrative – often for the first time. And in doing so, we hold space for joy, pride, and possibility.

But the ripples don't stop there. In the quiet corners of my life – the courtrooms where I advocate for foster children, the late-night texts from carers who need reassurance, the handwritten letters from former clients – I see how this way of showing up continues to echo.

Even in my own home, as a long-term foster carer, the same principles apply. Our house has held many young people – some for days, some for years. It's seen tears, tantrums, birthdays, breakdowns, breakthroughs. We don't promise perfection. But we promise presence. We promise to try again, to listen harder, to love without strings. That is our kind of peace.

It's easy to believe that peace is something passive – that it lives in monasteries or mountaintops. But I've learnt it's something we create, moment by moment, decision by decision. In how we speak. In how we listen. In how we show up, even when it's uncomfortable.

Holding space isn't glamorous. You won't find it on a list of KPIs. But it transforms everything it touches. Because when you truly see someone – and let them feel seen – you offer them the one thing every human craves: belonging.

That's the ripple I want to leave behind. Not a title. Not applause. But a wave of people who know how to hold space for others – and for themselves – with gentleness, grace and courage.

There was a time when I thought peace was something you found – and once found, you kept. Like a destination. A finish line. A reward for surviving enough hardship.

But peace, I've learnt, is not a place. It's a practice. A way of being in the world. It asks you to show up with softness, even when you've been hardened. It asks you to listen deeply, even when no one listened to you. It asks you to sit with discomfort, to unclench your fists, to hold space not only for others, but for yourself.

Peace is choosing presence over perfection. Curiosity over control. Love over fear.

I've lived through moments where peace felt impossible. Times when the weight of injustice, grief or exhaustion felt louder than hope. But even then – even in the quiet wreckage of it all – I found tiny fragments of peace: in the way someone held eye contact without flinching. In the way a child fell asleep safely under my roof. In the first sip of coffee after a long night. In a deep breath that said, 'I'm still here.'

Those moments became my practice. My lifeline.

And the more I leaned into them, the more I realised: we don't have to wait for the world to be peaceful in order to live peacefully. We can choose to be peace-bringers – in our homes, in our work, in the way we speak to ourselves and each other.

Every time we hold space – for a young person, a friend, a colleague, a stranger – we disrupt the noise of the world with presence. We interrupt shame with compassion. We offer healing, not through grand gestures, but through genuine connection.

And maybe that's the most powerful thing of all.

Because in the end, peace doesn't come from doing everything right. It comes from showing up with an open heart, a willing spirit and the courage to hold space for what's real.

If you take one thing from my story, let it be this:

You don't need to have all the answers. You don't need to fix everything. Just show up – with love, with integrity and with the willingness to listen.

That is the work.

That is the gift.

And that, I believe with my whole heart, is how we create peace – in our backyards, in our communities and in ourselves.

ABOUT SANDRA

A social entrepreneur, wellness advocate, award-winning author, speaker, professional youth practitioner and youth service consultant, fashion (runway and photographic) creative director and producer, experienced grooming and deportment educator and public relations/media consultant, Sandra is described by many as a humble leader, change maker and social justice advocate, with a wealth of knowledge and experience spanning across the not-for-profit, local and state government and business sectors, working in the youth, community and social services sector of australia for the past twenty-six years. sandra is employed full-time as a public servant, working full-time and undertaking various other volunteer roles within the community.

In 2015, Sandra co-founded Blue Beanie Projects, a registered health promotion charity aimed at reducing remote youth suicide rates and increasing regional and remote young people's access to professional, ethical and sustainable youth services. Blue Beanie work with young people to increase their social and emotional wellbeing, confidence, resilience, self-esteem and connection to community. Having lived and worked in some of Australia's most isolated and remote communities for most of her career, developing and implementing successful culturally appropriate youth service models, she is particularly experienced and a passionate advocate for service needs of young people and youth workers in remote areas and improving funding, training and resources for youth workers.

'I am extremely fortunate to have shared some of my greatest passions in life with my husband Dave, who is incredibly supportive of me. Together we co-founded Blue Beanie Projects; we co-owned and managed Soul Café in Karratha; and the most treasured joy of both of our lives are our children. We made a very conscious and well thought out decision many years ago to not have biological children. Together we chose to become foster carers. Through our work in community and youth services we saw the reality of children and teens without homes, moving between foster placements, group homes, crisis accommodation hostels and experiencing varying degrees of homelessness.

'It is what ultimately inspired us to become carers. We respect that this lifestyle choice is not for all families, but for us we asked why would we bring children into this world ourselves when there are so many children without homes and families already? People often ask us "why don't you have a family of your own?"; "don't you want to have your own kids?"; "why would you choose to take on other people's problems?" Our response is simple – our children, THEY ARE OUR OWN. We love them, care for them and will always be their mum and dad. You don't have to be biologically related to a child to call them your son or daughter. Family is so much more than biology, genetic makeup or DNA.

'As a mum, I raise my boys to be dreamers and believers; I want my boys to know that anything is possible for them and they can achieve anything they believe they can. We teach them every day, the importance of inclusivity, acceptance, understanding, empathy, kindness, speaking up for those who are silenced, gender diversity. The list is endless really, but the point is, each and every day we educate, mentor, guide, instil these very things into our children; all while balancing everyday life, work commitments, and above all keeping our boys connected to their Aboriginal culture, country and families. Educating them about Australian history and speaking to them of the truth of their ancestors, while continually reminding them of the resilience and courage of their people – those who walked before them for so many tens of thousands of years. Every day, building their pride, strength and ability to speak up even when their lips shake or their chins quiver. Teaching them to be advocates, social warriors and world changers.

'I love that these attributes and values are embodied not only in my youth work profession, but that I am able to weave them through my daily life, my friendships and with my family.'

SANJA & TOM HENDRICK
FLIPPING THE SCRIPT
HOW WE TURNED COMPETITION INTO COLLABORATION (AND ENDED UP MARRIED)

Sanja: 'Tom and I ran competing businesses as public speaking trainers.'

Tom: 'We've told this story on podcasts and at conferences so many times …'

Sanja: '… that when Cathy invited us to share it in a book, we knew we had to tell it exactly the way we always tell it.'

Tom: 'Which means you'll hear Sanja's version first, then mine, and then – just like our lives – you'll see where the stories meet in the middle.'

ACT 1: FROM BALLET TO BUSINESS TO BABIES (SANJA'S SIDE OF THE STORY)

Ever since I can remember, I loved the stage. Ballet was my first language. I like to joke that I was on pointe before I could walk.

As a teenager, I was auditioning for musical theatre roles when a lift went wrong. I was dropped from above a male dancer's head, damaging my lower back and – more heartbreakingly – my professional dance dreams.

Like a ballerina, I pivoted. I found ways to use my theatre skills in the corporate world, travelling around Australia with Commonwealth Bank's Start Smart program, teaching financial literacy in schools from a stage instead of a theatre.

During the Adelaide Fringe, I performed a show called Disney Diaries with a friend – an improvised hour of Disney princesses navigating modern problems. After one performance, a man approached me and asked: 'Could you teach my team to speak as confidently as you?'

His business card said 'Defence SA'. His question sparked the idea for my first business baby – Talent Academy.

For twelve years, I taught corporate professionals to present with theatre-inspired delivery skills. Where most coaches obsessed over slides and bullet points, I focused on the missing ingredient: confidence.

Then came 2020, and my life caught COVID. COVID shut down gatherings and my services became illegal overnight. My parents faced serious health issues. My long-term boyfriend walked out. My expensive five-year office lease kept bleeding money. I couldn't catch a break.

I felt like I was doing it alone.

And then came the hardest blow: at my annual health check, my fertility results were devastating – my AMH score was six. I re-tested: five. Another re-test: four. It was like a countdown.

At thirty-six, I was told I was close to perimenopause. I remember sitting in my car afterwards, too numb to cry. Too overwhelmed to move.

One year, multiple IVF scans and thousands of dollars later ... I had no baby and no viable business.

I decided to go out with a bang – a Christmas in July party where I'd announce I was shutting Talent Academy down. But COVID messed with that too.

It became a 'Christmas in July ... in August' party. After a glass (or three) of wine, I clinked a spoon on my glass and said: 'If I could have everyone's attention ... Talent Academy is shutting down. Let's celebrate while I commiserate.'

I don't regret sacrificing the business to help my family. But it felt like jumping off a bridge.

And that's when a hand grabbed mine and pulled me back onto solid ground.

That hand belonged to Tom – my direct competitor! Now, he's my business partner, husband and father of our two children. I like to say I acquired him in every sense of the word …

The point is: keeping my 'enemies' closer let me have my business and my family.

ACT 2: FROM COMEDY TO CORPORATE TO CO-FOUNDER (TOM'S SIDE OF THE STORY)

When I was thirteen, I had two much older brothers. Every night at the dinner table, my awkward teenage stories were drowned out by theirs.

My mum noticed me 'dribbling my words down my shirt', starting sentences but never finishing them. She decided to fix it.

Every Tuesday night, her elderly friend Hal – an ex-radio host – would visit with a yellowed book of tongue twisters and stories. He taught me how to speak with pace, tension, character and clarity.

Thanks to Hal, I won my first public speaking competition in year eight. Hal passed away before I could thank him, not just for helping me win, but for changing my life.

He'd taught me something I now call 'communication literacy' – the structures, patterns and artistry behind speaking.

I studied great communicators: comedians, politicians and TV hosts. I'd transcribe their words to uncover their patterns.

At eighteen, I studied law – a safe profession where I could talk a lot. I played it extra safe and decided to become a tax lawyer.

For twelve years, I buried my dream of being a public speaking coach under 'safe' choices. But not a day in twelve years went by that I didn't think: 'How can this be a business?'

One day, my brother announced at the dinner table that he was ending a seven-year relationship. We thought he would marry her. So I asked why, and he said: 'When the world's at war, you should want to be fighting with the person by your side. I didn't feel that way.'

I realised my 'safe decisions' were decisions made from fear. I ended my own 'safe but unhappy' long-term relationship, quit my law job and launched my speaking business.

I was going to do it all on my own.

A month later, I met with my friend Priya (a business coach) to sanity check my business model (after quitting my job ...). Priya said: 'You should meet Sanja from Talent Academy – you'd love her.' (Foreshadowing.) I already knew her – well, *of* her. She was at the top of my 'competitor analysis' file, with a note to 'copy and out-do her website'.

Priya invited me to Sanja's networking workshop. I hesitated – 'She'll think I'm stealing her material!' That was more of a confession than an excuse, but Priya twisted my arm and I went.

The first thing Sanja said when she saw me was: 'What are you doing here?!'

My panicked reply: 'I'm not here to steal your stuff ...' It wasn't love at first sight, yet – but fun fact: the word 'Priya' means 'love'. I like to think it was love that made me go.

Months later, I did steal something – Sanja's heart.

The point is: When I stopped fighting myself and others, I was able to meet who I was supposed to find.

ACT 3: FROM COMPETITORS TO COLLABORATORS TO COUPLE

Three hours after that workshop ended, we were the last two in the room, wine in hand and nerding out about communication philosophy.

Although the conversation between two public speaking coaches was awesome (go figure), we both were extremely cagey and dubious of the other, being direct competitors and all.

Sanja: 'Priya told me about you, but I couldn't find your website. No socials or anything about you.'

What Sanja did have was a team of six female business school interns co-authoring a document called 'competitor analysis'. It said: 'Former tax lawyer, no website, no socials … he would be cute if he shaved the beard off.' (True story.)

Tom: 'I quit my job as a lawyer to start a dream job last month. I've wanted to do this since I was thirteen years old. I've noticed a lot of public speaking coaches are from the theatre world, and I don't think they understand that corporate people want structure, not vocal exercises. It inspired me to believe I could start this business. Life has never been better, but I'm still finding my feet.'

Sanja, mortally offended by the slight on theatre people, politely continued the conversation: 'I've been doing this practically my whole life – theatre is my life. What are you working on?'

Tom: 'I'm trying to build networks, but it's weird. In the legal profession, everyone mingles. Even though you might be on different sides of a court case, you still say "Hi" and share ideas at networking events. But I've tried reaching out to a few public speaking coaches and … nothing. At best, I get ghosted; at worst, I get rejected. I was looking forward to finding someone I could share stories and communication philosophy with.'

Sanja: 'Well, we should take the advice from my workshop and find ways to collaborate instead of compete.'

The following week, we sat in Sanja's boardroom with a whiteboard, mapping out everything – markets, product ideas and networks. We walked away both energised and slightly terrified by how much we'd shared with a direct competitor.

But life had other plans.

Fast-forward to Sanja's shutdown party, where she announced that Talent Academy was closing. Tom's heart sank. He gave up everything for his dream and now couldn't stomach Sanja losing hers. He thought: *I want to go to war for this woman's dream.*

Tom offered to help Sanja save the business, not because of affection (that happened later) but because he could finally see himself in his competitor. He put his lawyer hat back on and negotiated her lease exit, ran workshops for her clients so she could go to medical appointments, and put his own dream business on hold to work for his competitor.

A week later, Sanja walked into the fertility clinic, and Tom was already there.

'What are you doing here?' That was the second time Sanja had said that to Tom in as many months.

'No one should go through this alone,' Tom replied.

That conversation turned into a bigger one about life, marriage and kids. By September, we'd decided we were all in –personally and professionally.

We met in June, collaborated in July, became co-directors in August, got engaged in November, became pregnant in December and married in February. In June, on the anniversary of the day we met, our first child was born (no IVF needed).

Today, Talent Academy is a team of ten, including seven former competitors who, like us, chose collaboration over competition.

None of this would have been possible without finding peace.

But because we were so busy fighting ourselves and each other, we needed serious luck to be this lucky.

If Sanja didn't extend the invitation to collaborate, if Priya didn't convince Tom to give his competitor a go, none of this would have happened.

In our experience, war is not the way to peace. When we stopped fighting ourselves and others, all that was left to 'fight for' were dreams and ideals.

ABOUT SANJA & TOM

Sanja and Tom Hendrick are the powerhouse duo behind **Talent Academy**, Adelaide's leading public speaking and performance training organisation. Together, they combine decades of experience in stagecraft, corporate training and professional speaking to help individuals and organisations communicate with confidence, clarity, and impact.

Sanja Hendrick, founder and managing director, is a public speaking coach, corporate MC, facilitator and speaker coach for TEDxUniSA. With over twenty years of theatre and screen experience, Sanja has trained speakers and leaders across Adelaide, Sydney, Melbourne and major cities in China. She is passionate about designing workshops that meet the unique needs of executives, managers and teams, creating engaging, outcome-driven sessions that help participants step into their power as communicators.

Tom Hendrick, director, brings a unique blend of corporate expertise and practical speaking strategies. A former tax lawyer with top-tier firm Finlaysons, Tom now runs Talent Academy's group workshops and one-to-one training. He works with government agencies, professional associations and businesses of all sizes to help speakers get a return on investment when they present, reduce preparation time and eliminate 'presentation dead space' by applying techniques used by world-class speakers.

Together, Sanja and Tom are passionate about building confidence in others, whether it's preparing a CEO for a keynote, coaching a manager for a board presentation or helping a young performer step onto the stage for the first time. Talent Academy is where people come to find their voice – and learn to use it powerfully.

talentacademy.com.au

SCOTT O'MEARA & BRITTA JENNINGS
FROM TOXIC BONDS TO SOULFUL LOVE

BRITTA ...

I grew up in a family where positive thinking, manifestation and alternative healing weren't just buzzwords – they were a way of life. These principles became my lifeline during some of my darkest moments as a child, helping me navigate sickness, bullying and the life stresses growing up.

By the time I was in my twenties, everything seemed to be falling perfectly into place. Every dream I had set my heart on was manifesting.

At just twenty years old, I landed my dream career in television –the only female producer in my department. With a lunchbox car packed full of everything I owned, I left my quiet beachside hometown for the bright lights of the big city.

And life didn't disappoint. Everything aligned so effortlessly – amazing flatmates, lifelong friendships, career success, property investment, new car, pay rises. I was building what I thought was the perfect foundation for my ultimate dream: a family.

But deep inside, I knew the city wasn't where I wanted to raise children. My career demanded long hours, and I longed for the peace of Noosa. So, I manifested working remotely – and the universe delivered.

At twenty-six, I gave birth to my first child. My heart exploded with a love I never knew existed. Becoming a mother cracked me wide open – but it also made me realise something painful: I had been settling for less, constantly people-pleasing and running myself into the ground to keep others happy.

That's when everything began to change.

I never imagined I would become a single mother – but life had other plans.

Suddenly, I was alone, with my little boy depending on me. This was the moment I first began to notice something deeper at play: limiting beliefs distorting my manifestations.

At the time, I couldn't see it clearly. But looking back, I know now that fears buried deep in my subconscious were shaping my reality. Fears of having more children and becoming a single mother again. Fears of rejection. Fears of not being enough.

Those fears intensified when I discovered I was carrying a sleeping baby – a devastating loss that broke me in ways I didn't know possible. From that pain came more limiting beliefs, and I now believe they blocked my ability to conceive again for years.

Women put enormous pressure on themselves to conceive, not realising how stress and fear can energetically shut down the process.

Eventually, I was blessed with another pregnancy – but complications shadowed every step. When my second son was born, he stopped breathing and had to be resuscitated; then the next couple of days were critical.

Then came my miracle: my daughter. Her arrival brought light back into my life, and for a while, things felt stable again.

Until the day I received a single text message that shattered everything.

It was from my children's father: 'I'm done. I'm through.'

In that moment, my world collapsed.

I was now a single mother of three beautiful children. Everything I had worked so hard for – financial security, career stability, the dream of a family – was gone. I went from being the breadwinner to financially vulnerable and emotionally broken.

I hit rock bottom.

I still remember lying on my bedroom floor, sobbing, praying to God, the universe, any higher power that would listen: 'Help me. I'm begging you for my children to get me through this.'

In that moment of surrender, something inside me ignited. I knew I had two choices as my mother would say: 'to sink or swim'. And I chose to swim – not just for me, but for my children.

That's when I discovered the power of subconscious limiting beliefs – the hidden programs running our lives without us even knowing. I realised that no matter how 'together' I looked on the outside, my subconscious was filled with fear-based scripts:

'I'm not good enough.'

'Love will always leave me.'

'I have failed at life.'

These beliefs weren't just shaping my reality – they were sabotaging it.

My first rejection limiting belief had formed in childhood when my best friend told me she couldn't be friends with someone who was sick for so long. That wound of rejection never healed. It grew deeper in high school when another best friend betrayed me, becoming my worst bully. And it didn't stop there. It showed up in relationships where I walked on eggshells, silenced my truth, and gave everything just to avoid rejection.

The patterns were undeniable:

More rejection.

More people-pleasing.

More self-abandonment.

The more I uncovered and released these limiting beliefs, the more my life began to transform.

I was no longer the terrified girl who fainted during a school presentation.

I was no longer the woman who lived for others while betraying herself.

I was no longer the soul who feared rejection so deeply she stayed in toxic relationships.

I reclaimed my voice.

I reclaimed my worth.

I reclaimed my life.

And from that place of power, I discovered my true purpose: helping others break free from the chains of their subconscious and create the life they truly deserve.

That's when I met my soulmate – someone who had walked his own path of pain and healing. Together, we combined our life experiences, spiritual wisdom and transformational tools to help thousands of people across the world heal and manifest their authentic life.

Because here's what I know for sure: No matter how broken you feel, your soul is never beyond repair.

Your past does not define your future.

And when you shift your subconscious, you don't just change your life – you rewrite your destiny.

SCOTT ...

As long as I can remember, I always wanted to help people – old people, animals and anyone who was bullied. I remember praying by my bed at the age of seven that I wanted to be an angel and help people, until my father walked in and said, 'What are you doing that for? That's nonsense.'

From that moment forward, I gave up on the idea of helping people. I listened to my father, who was very influential in my life.

I remember being a happy kid until I started becoming aware of my father's behaviour – being controlling, highly stressed and the way he spoke to my mother. I started to lose respect for him as a parent and became anxious and eventually depressed. I also lost a lot of self-confidence.

This affected every area of my life, all the way through to my dating life.

When I got to the age of dating, I started to realise that I felt unworthy of attracting love. After many years of relationships, I found I had a pattern of attracting the wrong women, but I wasn't sure why.

What I did know was that I was an empath, that I needed love to feel accepted and validated, and that I pushed away a lot of beautiful, loving, loyal women – while instead attracting troubled women who were often narcissistic by nature. Throughout my dating years, I lost my identity and sense of purpose.

At nineteen, I decided to get back to helping people. I joined the police service so I could help people and to become that angel again.

I was involved in a stabbing incident at work and developed PTSD. From there, I hit an all-time low, abusing ecstasy and cocaine to self-medicate as I was severely depressed. I was then led into the bright lights and high-energy music of the Sydney nightlife, where I found solace with people who were going through the same thing as me.

I hit rock bottom after a breakup. In this relationship, I was controlled, emotionally and physically abused, and made to feel worthless. After I moved out, I was hit with a sudden attack of depression. This heavy energy came over me like I'd never felt before. It was so paralysing that I was lying on the floor, unable to move. It was impossible to shake this feeling. I was never more scared in my life.

I never understood why someone would want to commit suicide – until then. For the first time ever, I felt so paralysed and hopeless that I could see no way out. All I knew was that I had to get out of this pain. I looked towards the sky and yelled out, 'If there is a God, come and save me now because I need you more than ever!'

Instantly, the pain and the thoughts slowly subsided. Afterward, it was clear that all I had to do was ask God and the universe for help, and

I would receive it. It confirmed for me that God is real.

This made me realise that if God is real and He can help me with this, then He can help me with the rest of my life. So I started asking for more healing and help.

Shortly after, I met an amazing lady who was my friend's new girlfriend.

Leisa was a spiritual coach and she helped me find myself again. But really, the most powerful and profound healing came when she reprogrammed my limiting beliefs. Instantly, I felt an enormous heavy energy lift.

She taught me that through connection to a higher source and by surrendering my trauma, I could heal instantly – and that we are only limited by our beliefs, including who we attract. This was profound. I now had the secret to life and further confirmation that I could call upon the universe at any time to help and heal. All I had to do was ask, and it would be given.

After I rapidly healed, I started my coaching business to help people just like me.

Next on the agenda was to attract my soulmate – a compatible soulmate who shared my vibration. So what did I do? I asked the universe to bring her to me within the next twelve weeks. I even wrote a list of everything I wanted in a soulmate.

I met my soulmate three days short of the twelve weeks – at a barbecue.

Thanks, universe!

Fast-forward: My partner, Britta, and I have worked with over six thousand clients all around the world to help people grow and heal from toxic and narcissistic relationships, teaching them how to manifest true love and become their most authentic selves.

We have created a proven healing journey based on years of experience and wisdom. Together, our mission is to help over one million people heal from relationships and find their soulmates.

What we've learnt from helping all these people is this: It doesn't matter what pain you're experiencing or what you need to heal – connecting with God/universe/creator/higher source and being vibrationally aligned with what you want to attract is all you need.

How you appear in the mirror, how you look at yourself, how you feel, and the beliefs you hold about who you are – all dictate who and what you attract into your life. Do you attract love, abundance, happiness and joy? Or do you attract trauma and sabotage your life?

We discovered that there are six healing phases that people need to go through to truly heal:

PHASE 1: GET CLARITY

Clarity is needed to start the process of healing and creation. It is important to know where you are right now and where you want to go.

This is pivotal in manifesting healing and the life you want.

We don't enter this world burdened with doubt or fear – we come in as a blank canvas. But from the moment we are conceived, we begin absorbing the energy, beliefs and patterns of those around us. If we weren't planned or fully welcomed, we might unconsciously take on beliefs like 'I am unworthy' or 'I don't belong'. As life unfolds, layers of trauma, drama and pain from parents, peers and personal experiences further shape our sense of self.

These beliefs become the lenses through which we see the world – and ourselves. The good news? They are not permanent. Once we uncover these hidden weaknesses, rewrite them into strengths and reconnect with who we truly are, transformation begins. That's why phase two is so essential – it's where the real shift happens.

PHASE 2: IDENTIFY AND REPROGRAM LIMITING BELIEFS

We create our belief systems predominantly from childhood trauma and experiences.

Main limiting beliefs that affect who you attract include:

'I am not worthy of love.'

'There is no soulmate out there for me.'

'I'm afraid of rejection.'

'I attract narcissistic partners.'

These beliefs subconsciously create an energetic frequency that determines the relationships you attract. By rewiring these beliefs from negative to positive, you can dramatically change who you attract.

Example: Our client, Sam, attracted two narcissistic men – one relationship even put her in a coma. After helping her heal and change her belief system, she attracted her soulmate – a kind, gentle, loving man – within twelve weeks.

PHASE 3: DETACHMENT

We help clients detach from trauma and narcissists so they stop going back to them and can heal properly. This involves returning soul fragments and reclaiming personal power.

PHASE 4: SPECIALISED HEALING

To truly transform, you need a specific, targeted healing journey that addresses the root cause of the problem. Most trauma goes back to childhood – even to the womb. If we don't heal properly, we can pass trauma and beliefs on to our children, continuing the cycle of toxic relationships.

PHASE 5: MANIFEST

We are all powerful manifestors. It's about clarity, intention, asking the universe, removing blocks and being ready to receive – while staying vibrationally aligned.

Example: Our client Pam asked if she could manifest a soulmate at seventy-three. I said, 'Yes, as long as you surrender, heal and allow the universe/God to bring it to you.' Six months later, she called to say she was engaged to a beautiful man.

PHASE 6: ACCOUNTABILITY, STRATEGY AND MEASURABILITY

Most people can't measure their healing journey, but this is paramount.

We help clients track progress and celebrate wins.

Example: Trudy, forty-six, wanted a baby but kept attracting men who only used her for sex. She had three eggs left and was desperate. After clearing her blocks and fears, she met her soulmate within three months – and now has a beautiful baby boy.

When you have dominant fears and insecurities, you attract more of them through the law of attraction.

The biggest lesson from our spiritual journey is this: Live your most authentic life. If a doctor told you that you have three weeks to live, would you be satisfied with the life you've been living and who you've become? Most people would say no.

Too often, we prioritise money, material things and careers over family, love and happiness. True success in life is finding yourself, loving yourself and creating from that space of alignment with the universe.

You can't buy happiness – you can only *be* happiness. This is your chance, your opportunity, to create all the happiness and joy you desire – because you are worth it.

ABOUT SCOTT & BRITTA

Scott and Britta are the co-founders of Relationship Warrior and are passionate about helping women and men to heal from toxic and narcissistic relationships and to be their authentic self and find their true purpose in this life and attracting true love.

SHARON JONES
HEALING FROM WITHIN
HOW I RECLAIMED MY BODY AND MY POWER

OPENING SCENE: WHO ARE YOU?

There was a moment when I sat quietly on my living room floor, tears tracing familiar paths down my face as I stared blankly at the list of medical terms I barely understood. 'Ankylosing spondylitis,' my doctor had said, his voice calm and clinical. My body, however, felt like it was screaming. My spine felt fused with fire, and every movement reminded me of what I had lost: freedom, certainty and even trust in my own body.

But what no one saw in that moment was the silent vow I made to myself: This is not where my story ends.

At that point, I had spent years pushing through relentless pain, trying to stay strong while juggling work, responsibilities and the exhausting task of appearing 'fine'. The world kept moving, but I had stopped.

What I didn't realise then was that this diagnosis would become my invitation – not to break down, but to break open.

This is the story of how I reclaimed my body, my voice and my power – and how every woman navigating autoimmune illness can do the same. This is for the woman lying in bed, wondering if she'll ever feel like herself again. For the warrior whose labs don't show the whole story. For the one who's silently carrying pain in her bones, but strength in her heart.

You don't have to walk this path alone. Healing from autoimmune disease is hard – but it's possible. You already have the strength inside you. My journey is simply a mirror for your own.

THE BEFORE: LIVING IN THE FOG

Before I embraced healing, I lived in survival mode.

Each morning was a question mark. Would I be able to get out of bed without collapsing in pain? Could I trust my body enough to make plans or, worse, cancel them again and explain why I had to? My identity, once rooted in capability and care for others, felt buried under chronic inflammation and invisible symptoms.

Autoimmune disease has a way of making you feel erased. People around you don't see the fatigue that hits like a freight train after brushing your teeth. They don't feel the internal war your body wages on itself. They can't hear the ache in your soul as your world shrinks around your limitations.

I spent years trying to 'fix' myself through outside means: doctors, diets, pushing harder, pretending it wasn't that bad. But nothing stuck. I was doing all the right things and still getting worse.

What no one tells you is that healing doesn't start with a plan. It starts with a pause.

It wasn't until I hit complete burnout that I finally realised what I needed wasn't more control. It was compassion. I needed to stop fighting my body and start listening to her.

And when I began to listen, I heard something profound.

She wasn't broken. She was begging to be heard.

THE TURNING POINT: WHEN I CHOSE MYSELF

The moment of shift wasn't dramatic. There was no lightning bolt or overnight cure. It was a quiet realisation, after yet another day spent in pain, that I was tired of abandoning myself.

Instead of asking, 'Why is my body doing this to me?' I began asking, 'What is my body trying to tell me?'

That one question changed everything.

It led me to explore the mind-body connection, not as a vague concept, but as a real, physiological truth. I discovered how trauma, stress and even unprocessed emotions were deeply entangled in my physical pain. I stopped seeing my diagnosis as the enemy and started seeing it as a messenger.

Slowly, I began building a new relationship with myself. I started saying 'no' to things that depleted me and 'yes' to what nourished me. I swapped perfectionism for progress, punishment for presence.

I invested in therapy, movement, nourishment and – most powerfully – community. I reached out to other women living with chronic illness. I realised I wasn't alone and that maybe, just maybe, my story could help someone else heal, too.

That was the spark. And it has never gone out.

THE JOURNEY: REBUILDING FROM WITHIN

Recovery didn't come wrapped in a single answer. It came in layers, slowly and steadily.

I started with the smallest things: drinking water before coffee, breathing intentionally for five minutes, and learning to rest without guilt. These 'small' actions were radical acts of self-love in a world that taught me to ignore my body's needs.

Then I got curious about what actually supported my body's healing.

I eliminated inflammatory foods and learnt to tune into my gut – not just my literal gut, but my intuition. I practised gentle movement, even if it was just stretching in bed. I found joy again in creativity and connection. And I created rituals around sleep, nourishment and self-care that felt like love letters to myself.

The biggest shift came when I began to trust my body again. Not as something to be managed, but as a partner.

I journaled. I cried. I forgave myself for not knowing better. I celebrated my wins – getting dressed, making a meal and walking outside. Every 'small' step was a big one when chronic illness had once stolen so much.

Through this process, I stopped waiting to be 'fixed' and began living again.

And the more I healed, the more I was called to help others do the same.

That's when my coaching practice was born; not from theory, but from lived experience. I became the support I once wished I had; someone who understood the layers of healing, someone who wouldn't flinch at the words 'I'm not okay.'

Today, I help women with autoimmune and chronic conditions reclaim their health; not with quick fixes, but with compassion, strategy and community.

Healing from within is not linear. But it is possible.

And you're not too late.

THE TRANSFORMATION: RESILIENCE RECLAIMED

Now, I live in partnership with my body.

Do I still have symptoms? Sometimes. But they no longer own me. I have tools, boundaries and deep trust in my body's signals. I work with her, not against her. And that changes everything.

The most powerful transformation wasn't physical; it was emotional.

I began to see my illness as a sacred teacher. It taught me how to slow down, to listen, to be soft with myself. It taught me that strength isn't pushing through pain, it's choosing rest. It's choosing you.

THE BACKYARD PEACE PROJECT: VOL 1

I now live with more intention, clarity and joy than I ever thought possible. I'm building a life around alignment, not achievement. I've created a coaching business that allows me to help others rise, not just despite their diagnoses, but because of what they've discovered in the process.

You don't have to be 'healed' to live fully. You just have to be willing to meet yourself where you are, with love.

I'm not the same woman who sat crying on her living room floor. I'm someone who trusts her body. Who holds space for others. Who believes that every woman deserves to feel powerful in her own skin again.

And so do you.

YOUR MESSAGE TO THE READER: AN INVITATION

Dear warrior,

If you're reading this and feel like your world has gotten smaller since your diagnosis, I want you to know this:

You are not alone.

You are not broken.

And your healing is not behind schedule.

You have everything you need within you to begin again. It starts with one decision: to believe in your body's wisdom and your right to thrive.

I see you. I believe in you. And I am here for you.

If you're ready to reclaim your life and step into a new chapter of healing, I invite you to connect with me. Whether through one-on-one coaching or group sessions, you don't have to walk this path alone.

Let's rewrite your story, together.

With resilience and warmth,

Sharon Jones

Resilience Coach | Autoimmune Warrior

ABOUT SHARON

I'm Sharon, a resilience life coach living with ankylosing spondylitis, and I specialise in supporting people with autoimmune conditions. After years of pain, uncertainty and spinal surgery, I chose not to let my diagnosis define me, and instead, I reclaimed my power and turned my experience into purpose.

Through my coaching program, Empowered Pathways, I offer practical tools, compassionate support and mindset strategies to help you navigate chronic illness with more ease, clarity and confidence.

This journey isn't about quick fixes; it's about finding strength in your story and creating a life that feels aligned, joyful and empowered.

I'm here to walk alongside you.
sharonj.coach@gmail.com

STEPHANIE VAUGHAN
FINDING STRENGTH THROUGH STYLE

At the age of forty-one, life was good. All three of my children were at school, and my husband had a great job. I had a casual position in a women's fashion store which I loved, and I was enjoying the lifestyle we had created for our family. I also had a great network of friends, including several mums from school, who were all very social, organising everything from coffee mornings to putting a social netball team together.

A few weeks into the season, I remember standing on a netball court and feeling a strange sensation in my left hand. It was the first time I had felt it. I thought maybe the flu shot I'd had the day before had hit a nerve. When the unusual movement and feeling hadn't subsided after a few days, I went to see my GP, thinking it was odd.

I sat and explained why I was there, and the doctor printed out a referral to see a neurologist without any explanation. I thought he was sending me there for no real reason other than the possibility of some kind of nerve damage. I arranged for my parents to come and look after my three young children so that I could go to the appointment. That morning, I had thoughts of cancelling, feeling like I was going to be spending money unnecessarily and wasting everyone's time. The kids were looking forward to seeing their grandparents, so I decided to go along.

I went alone, still feeling slightly guilty about taking up the neurologist's time. I arrived at his rooms feeling as though he was going to tell me I was being overly dramatic and that the strange sensation and movement would eventually settle.

After a short wait, I was called into his office and took a seat across from him. He was seated behind his big desk, reading notes on his desktop. I cannot recall any conversation as such, but I remember thinking he was going to tell me that I just needed to give my arm time to settle, and there was no reason for me to be seeing him.

I had only been in there a couple of minutes before, from what felt like out of nowhere, I was asked the question: 'So, what are we going to do about your Parkinson's?'

I had no idea what he was talking about. There had been no mention of this from my GP, and it wasn't even on my radar. It took me a while to even register what he had said. I was totally blindsided. I knew nothing about Parkinson's other than it was an 'old person's disease' and I had recently heard that Michael J Fox had been diagnosed with it. I also knew that there was no cure for Parkinson's disease.

The rest of the consultation was a blur. There was mention of medication and an MRI, and I was handed the details of a local support group for people with Parkinson's. When I left, I got as far as crossing the road but couldn't make it to my car, so I just sat myself down on the side of the road in the gutter. I wasn't ready to go home. I knew there would be questions about my appointment as my parents were naturally concerned and would want to know what was going on.

While sobbing uncontrollably, I called my husband, who was at work, and tried to tell him what I had just been told. He came straight away, picked me up from the gutter I was still sitting in, and helped me to the car. We drove to a quiet cafe nearby, and I recounted my appointment and what I could remember of the diagnosis delivery. Eventually, I got myself together and we headed home.

THE BACKYARD PEACE PROJECT: VOL 1

The kids were excited to see us both home, and I could see that my parents wanted to know what was happening. I waited until the kids had gone off to play in their rooms and then broke the news to Mum and Dad. They were both as shocked and devastated as I was, but they were also supportive and understanding when I said that I wasn't ready to let the kids know. I didn't want to scare them and wanted to tell them in my own time and way. There wasn't a lot to discuss at that stage anyway, as I had no idea what to think and needed time to process.

The one thing I remember most from that conversation was my parents saying they wouldn't tell anyone, which I was fine with. But in that moment, for some strange reason, a feeling of shame crept in, and my diagnosis had now become a secret. My parents loved me, and I knew they were being respectful of this being my news to share if I wished to, but that feeling of shame just grew to the point that I didn't want to tell anyone that I had an 'old person's disease' at the age of forty-one. I was worried that if I told people, they would judge me or feel pity for me. I didn't want this disease to define me.

I broke the news of my diagnosis to the kids in my own way, very gently, and reassured them that it was nothing for them to be worried about. They took it well, which was a relief, and for them life went on as normal … but not for me. My world had totally changed. It was dark and lonely. I had a secret. I didn't want anyone to see me. I felt shame. I was embarrassed that I had an 'old person's disease'. I had no idea what to expect or how to manage this uninvited beast.

There's no way of knowing where or when a new symptom will show up, it has a mind of its own, which makes it hard when you're looking at planning your future.

On the outside, I just kept living life as normal. Nobody knew a thing. But on the inside, I was full of fear and shame and was grieving the loss of feeling normal. My husband, kids and parents were the only ones who knew about my diagnosis for quite a while.

I went back to the neurologist and, as much as I pushed against it, I reluctantly started on medications. Deciding to go along to the support group I still had the details for, I sought advice from others who were also dealing with life with Parkinson's. It was nothing like I had expected.

When I walked in, I was the youngest in the room. Nobody smiled, there was no conversation, and there were several people smoking in the room. I must have looked surprised to see so many people smoking, as one of the staff (who was a nurse) went on to tell me that smoking was good for people with Parkinson's, as it helped keep stress levels down. I immediately excused myself and got the hell out of there.

I had a handful of brochures and a booklet on how to manage life with Parkinson's, which I'd been given when I first arrived, so later that night I decided to read through them. It was full of advice for older people, but there was nothing at all to represent my age group. I jumped onto Google and went down the rabbit hole, reading everything I could around the latest research and self-help methods others were trying.

I knew from all that I'd read that exercise was super important, so I turned my regular post-school drop-off beach walk, into an intermittent walk and jog, which eventually became a morning run. I found solace through running. I was in control. I could release my anger, and nobody questioned my new-found obsession. Running was my new friend. I would roll out of bed before dawn to get in several kilometres before taking the kids to school and then do a few more after drop-off. I went on an exercise journey in the hope of reversing or stalling the disease. It made me feel good.

I also felt good on the days I went to work. Working in fashion was the perfect excuse for me to dress up and wear clothes that I loved and that made me feel like myself again. I noticed that on the days I dressed for work, I felt confident and could show up as the person I wanted to be.

My clothes were my armour; they protected me and uplifted me at the same time. On the days I wasn't working, I didn't feel as great, which

I took note of. I also loved the fashion and the women who came in to shop. I was always in my element when I was styling customers in outfits that made them walk out feeling and looking amazing.

Nobody knew about my diagnosis besides my family and a handful of my closest friends. Working in the store one morning, one of the girls I was working with had noticed my tremor.

During a quiet moment, she asked me about it. I couldn't bring myself to tell her the truth. Fear of being defined by this disease held me back, so I told her it was the result of too much caffeine, which we then joked about – I was in the clear. I didn't like that I was hiding the truth from people, but I wasn't ready to accept my diagnosis.

I had learnt to hide and manage my tremor, which was still only in my left hand, but then suddenly, while driving, I noticed a strange movement and sensation in my left leg. It had spread.

I went back to my neurologist, and he confirmed my fear: it was progressing. Not knowing what type or when any other symptoms might start to present themselves, I felt as though I was a ticking time bomb. It became clear that whatever I wanted to do in life, getting on and just doing it while I could was the only way to go.

This feeling of needing to do something more with my life, to follow my passion for both style and helping others, manifested in my personal styling career. After doing a lot of soul searching and research, I found a stylist in Melbourne who ran certified training courses in personal style. Booking the course and a plane ticket, I headed to Melbourne for the course. I had found my calling. I didn't just feel good about myself, I felt I had purpose again.

With my certificate behind me, I founded Infinite Styling in 2013. I had no idea how to run a business; it was a whole new world I was stepping into. It felt both overwhelming and exciting at the same time. I started out slowly, doing shopping sessions and wardrobe edits for friends, which was perfect practise while I was finding my feet. I joined a couple of business groups and started heading out to women's networking events, where I began to find a few clients.

While I was feeling my way along, an opportunity came up for an internship to assist the fashion editor with a local magazine, *South Australian Style*. I applied and won the position. This was perfect as the magazine was a quarterly issue, so I could keep working on my business. I learnt and experienced so much, from editorial styling work to fashion events, photoshoots on location and working with a few local celebrities. I loved working alongside the fashion editor and after a couple of issues, I was hired as assistant to the fashion editor, which I just loved.

The creativity of pulling outfits together from around a hundred stores for advertising purposes was always fun, but sometimes challenging, as was the physical side of selecting, collecting, shooting and returning everything. I hadn't shared that I had Parkinson's, so I had to work extra hard to hide my tremor, which was more difficult when I was feeling tired.

I started to notice my body changing again, but this time it was my movement and fine motor skills that were becoming a challenge. I was suddenly struggling to do up buttons and clips on accessories, and I could feel a slight shuffle with my walking. A visit to my neurologist confirmed that I was experiencing dyskinesia, which causes involuntary movements and muscle contractions and can affect speaking and moving.

I noticed that tiredness and stress exaggerated my symptoms, so along with a few changes to my medications, I decided I needed to focus on looking after myself more. As much as I loved working with the magazine, I stepped out of my role and put all my focus back into my styling business. I went back to doing my early morning runs, eating and sleeping properly, and listening to my body more than I had been before.

With a desire to build my business, as it had just been ticking along quietly while I was with the magazine, I went along to as many events and workshops as I could to both network and learn more about all things business. One particular event, however, turned out to be a complete game changer.

I went along to a free four-hour workshop which was presented by an amazing lady, Marnie, from Perth, who was touring the country to do speaking and sign-ups for her business coaching.

Everything she spoke about completely resonated with me, and at the end of the session, I took a massive leap and signed up for twelve months of coaching, which meant a few trips to Perth for small in-house group workshops and online coaching.

What I hadn't realised was that the workshops were all personal development seminars. It was something so new to me, but I loved it. At the very beginning of the first workshop, I filled in a form where I mentioned I had Parkinson's, as for some reason I felt they should know.

On the second-to-last day of the seminar, we all had to get up and speak about ourselves, what challenges we wanted to address, and which word best described how we were emotionally feeling. The word I chose was 'shame', which I soon discovered is the lowest emotional vibration scale.

I was the last one to speak, and when it was my turn, Marnie came up to the front and stood behind me. Just when I thought I had finished, she asked what one challenge was holding me back from being authentically me. I couldn't answer. She knew that I'd been secretly living with Parkinson's because I had asked for it to be kept confidential after handing her my registration form. She asked me again. I knew then what she was doing: she was holding space for me to finally give myself permission to be free of my secret. She asked once more, and I shouted the three words I didn't want to come out, 'I have Parkinson's!'

It was like a super strong energy had just been released, and she encouraged me to shout it out several times. It felt big, as I had been hiding not only from everyone around me but also from myself. It had been eight years since my initial diagnosis, and I hadn't realised until then that I had been sitting in shame all this time. I was ashamed of this disease and I was ashamed of not being honest with people if they questioned my tremor. I had discovered how to lean into personal style to be the person I wanted to be on the outside, but on the inside, while some days my outfits made me feel strong and unstoppable, there were still times when I didn't want anyone to see the real me.

My secret was finally out, my fear of being judged by the other women in the room quickly disappeared, and instead I was surrounded by love and support. I felt oddly different afterwards, and for the following few weeks, I experienced what I can only really describe as a healing process after eight years of hiding. For a while, tears would suddenly come up from nowhere whenever I took a shower, like my body was releasing the shame I had carried for so long. I felt like I had taken the first few steps of allowing myself to be me again.

Over the next few weeks, and then months, I slowly settled into acceptance, feeling better within myself, working on self-love and confidence. I had also been encouraged to tell my story, not only as part of my healing journey but also to help and inspire others who were experiencing their own journey. It was the week before my fiftieth birthday that I finally wrote and shared my story with the world on social media. After nine years of hiding, I decided it was time. It was actually this quote that made my decision: 'Strength through vulnerability'. These few words spoke to me and became my personal mantra.

My styling business is my 'why'. I now work predominantly with women, helping them to step into their own personal power through authentic personal style, and it is seeing them shine that lights me up and brings me the most joy. Realising that everyone has something, whether it's a health issue or something else in life that has rocked their confidence, it is my mission to help other women see their beauty and embrace who they truly are. Style is not superficial; it's soul work.

ABOUT STEPHANIE

Stephanie Vaughan, an inspired stylist, discovered the importance of personal style through her own life experience. At forty-one, she faced a life-changing health diagnosis, taking her down a path of self-discovery through style. Realising that the right outfit can be uplifting, even on the most challenging days, it became her mission to empower others to regain their confidence and reflect their true self.

Having worked in the fashion retail industry for many years, Stephanie undertook formal training to become a certified personal stylist, to further her knowledge and skills to turn her passion for styling into her career. In 2013, she launched her own styling business, Infinite Styling, and has been helping women to find and fall in love with their style again ever since.

As a stylist, Stephanie has also worked in editorial styling, taking on a role as assistant fashion editor for South Australian Style magazine, along with commercial styling for advertising campaigns and branding.

With well over fifteen years of experience as a stylist, Stephanie has worked with hundreds of women, both one-on-one and through workshop events, helping them to step into their own personal power through authentic and intuitive style.

infinitestyling.com.au

VIRGINIE ESPRIT
THREADS OF LOVE
BREAKING THE CYCLE OF TRAUMA

By the sound of my mother's high heels walking up to our home from work, I knew whether I was going to be in trouble that day or not …

East Germany, 1988. It was a picturesque winter morning, the air crisp and clear, as the season of Christmas approached. Every window displayed traditional lit candle arches of all makes, colours and sizes. It was magical. The soft glow of these candles was mesmerising, creating a sense of wonder that lasted from the end of November through to mid-January. I had my very own candle arch sitting proudly on the windowsill of my room. To turn it off, you simply unscrewed one of the light bulbs slightly, causing the rest of the lights to go out.

I was seven years old when I did just that. My mother had already left the house for work that morning, and I was waiting for the moment when I could leave for school. I would always wave goodbye to her from my bedroom window and watch her walk until she disappeared from my sight. I knew I wasn't allowed to play with the lights like that, but the fascination was too strong for me to resist. I twisted the bulbs, watching the lights flicker on and off. About five minutes later, I saw my mother walking briskly toward our apartment building, her face tense with anger. I froze.

I heard the front door slam open. She rushed into my room, grabbed me by the arm, yanked me from the window, threw me onto the ground and began to beat me with her hands and feet. I curled into a foetal position, knees pressed tightly to my chest, arms covering my head, doing my best to protect myself from the blows. I was terrified, screaming in pain, begging her to stop. She screamed at me, accusing me of being the reason she was going to be late for work, blaming me for making her miss the bus because she had to 'teach me a lesson'. Her rage escalated with every word, and there was nothing I could do except endure it, waiting for the storm to pass.

It was just another day in my life. If it wasn't the candle arch, it was my beloved budgie who kept escaping his cage in my room. Or me voicing an opinion. Or simply breathing the wrong way.

My father never knew any of this. At least, that's what I believe. He worked long hours at the city's coal processing plant, ensuring that our town had electricity every day. When he came home at the end of the day, I would tell him how my mother had beaten me, and she would call me a liar in front of him. She played the victim, accusing me of fabricating horrible stories about her.

My father, always torn between loyalty to me and his wife, would stand paralysed by overwhelm. He never got involved but always sided with my mother. I understand now why he acted this way; he too, was under my mother's controlling abuse. However, back then, it made me feel alone. Incredibly alone.

I grew up believing I was a terrible person. I heard it every day. I was a nuisance to my mother, a burden she couldn't bear. She threatened to send me to foster care on more than one occasion because she couldn't deal with me. What made me so difficult to deal with? I didn't know. I never knew what I did wrong. I didn't want to upset anyone, especially my mum. I loved my mother. And you don't hurt people you love, right?

The hostile environment I grew up in shaped the way I viewed myself and my relationships. The trauma I experienced became deeply ingrained, leaving me with a lifetime of responses and coping mechanisms I had learned to survive. It was a world filled with hostility and constant threats, filled with emotional and physical abuse.

And as I would come to learn much later, I was also born into a family with a profound legacy of trauma passed down through generations. My great-grandparents and grandparents were children of World Wars I and II. And no-one who lived through those times came out unscathed. My great-grandmother, whom I loved dearly, endured horrific sexual assault by soldiers who invaded her home village in Hungary. She was violently separated from her husband, who was sent to fight the war, and she was forced to board a train to East Germany, a country where she didn't speak the language, while nursing her little daughter, my grandmother.

My family carried the deep-seated trauma of those who had lived through unimaginable loss, war and repression. My body bore the scars of those unhealed wounds, as did my relationships, my emotions and my life. Everything was a mess until much later, when I started healing the inherited traumas I carried, and finally partnered with myself, unconditionally.

It took many years for me to heal, as I did it alone. I had no mentor to guide me through the process of breaking unhealthy family dynamics. I was left to figure it all out on my own. I didn't know what to do with the hostility and violence that surrounded me, but I knew I had to heal it.

In every corner of my family, immediate and extended, there was trauma and drama. Yet, woven throughout that painful history, there was a thread. A thin but unbreakable thread. Spun and held together by my great-grandmother and grandmother, whom I adored, this thread was strong. This thread was … love. Pure, unwavering love. A love carried in my foremothers' veins, so powerful that nothing could touch it. No matter how much the war, the abusive family members, the soldiers or the political regime tried to beat it out of them, it remained untouchable. They loved, regardless, despite it all, or perhaps because of it. Either way, it was there.

My mother was not part of that thread. She got lost along the way, consumed by the pain of her own trauma. My grandmothers passed on that thread of love to me, and I never let go of it. I held onto it, it was anchored deeply in my heart, even though I didn't fully understand its significance until much later in life. It was that very thread of love that guided me through my childhood and later through my healing journey.

I grew up in post-war communist East Germany, a world that was divided both geographically and emotionally. My parents were children of the Cold War, born into a world shaped by the brutal aftermath of two world wars. My Hungarian grandmother's family had been scattered across the globe during the Second World War. Some were sent to America and others were relocated to Germany. The missing limbs and mental health challenges suffered by my forefathers and foremothers were a testament to the harsh times they endured.

The fall of the Iron Curtain in 1989 was a pivotal moment in history, and I was just a young girl when the Berlin Wall came down. This event marked the end of the physical and ideological division between the communist east and the democratic west. It was a moment in history that not only reshaped Europe but also had a profound impact on my own path, one I could never have imagined at the time. With both of my parents rebelling against the communist regime, that day represented more than the reunion of a divided Germany and a transition from an authoritarian regime to a functioning democracy. It was symbolic of freedom, the right to walk freely, the right to choose what to eat, what to think, what to wear, which news to listen to and which profession to pursue. It was the right to express yourself without fear of public degradation or imprisonment.

Growing up in an atmosphere of fear, repression and violence, I learned that emotions were dangerous. Expressing anger, seeking help or showing vulnerability was met with suppression, so I learned to suppress my own feelings and numb myself to the pain by becoming a source of constant positivity and servitude, hoping to turn conflict into harmony. It was a survival mechanism that worked for a time but was certainly not sustainable.

Yet, even throughout this turmoil, I felt a deep connection to something beyond this world. I often felt out of place, different from the other children around me. My interests, my spirituality and my curiosity about the universe and extraterrestrial life set me apart. I would look up at the stars every night, feeling a deep sense of homesickness for a place I couldn't remember, yet knew so well. This sense of being different, of being disconnected, only intensified the trauma I carried. But it also led me to question the world around me, to look for answers beyond the physical realm.

My journey began in my early teens, when my mother fell into a coma after a stroke, and I was forced to confront the reality of her trauma. Her psychological struggles, her emotional pain and her inability to heal from her past became a family secret. During this time, I was introduced to the world of psychology. The books my mother brought home from her therapy sessions sparked my curiosity, and I became deeply fascinated by human psychology. It was a 'secret world', and I was hooked.

This spark of curiosity ignited the beginning of my personal transformation. It led me on a path of self-discovery and healing. I began to study the mind, body and spirit connection, diving deep into the world of spirituality and the study of trauma, psychology, neuroscience and energy healing. I explored vibrational medicine, heart-brain coherence, meditation practices, epigenetics, neuroscience, Buddhism and psychoanalysis, and so much more. I learned how our bodies hold onto past trauma, and more importantly, how we can heal it. How we can reprogram the wounds of the past with love, compassion and peace.

Through my studies, I began to unravel the layers of fear and pain that had been ingrained in me. I learned to embrace the person I was meant to be, beyond the fear and the limitations that had been placed upon me.

As I embarked on my healing journey, my meditation practices deepened, and I began to establish connections with something beyond this world. Through these connections, I expanded my awareness and embraced the guidance I was receiving from 'higher realms'. In silent meditation, I reconnected with source energy and its infinite wisdom that transcended time and space, offering profound insights that supported my healing process. These experiences also helped me understand the greater cosmic context of our lives and how interconnected we all are, not just with one another, but with the universe itself.

However, amongst this transformational journey I was on, I still hadn't figured out the most important thing of all. Self-love! I knew of it. Every text and study I consumed wrote about the importance of self-love. But how does one embody self-love?

The lack of self-love was evident in every single one of my relationships. From the get-go, domestic violence, dysfunctional family relationships and the general lack of emotional intelligence in my upbringing left me unprepared for healthy connections. I wasn't set up to succeed; I was set up to fail in all of my relationships. And for years, I repeated patterns of toxic relationships, not just in romantic partnerships, but in all areas of my life. I found myself drawn to environments of emotional chaos, whether in work, friendships or intimate relationships. This was the conditioning of my past: I was seeking familiarity, not love, not peace, not respect.

Chasing that thin thread of love in my relationships, I poured myself into them, loving with all my heart and believing that love could heal everything. I tried to fix people, seeing only their potential and hoping they could see it too. I was in relationships with their potential, not with who they truly were. This is how I escaped the pain of abuse and dysfunction. In psychology, this is known as a trauma response called dissociation. My world of potential was a beautiful one, filled with unconditional love, supportive communities and respect for all life. It was a place where people and animals lived in harmony with the great intelligence of the universe, humming 'hakuna matata' around a campfire somewhere.

But this inability to face reality, combined with my deep desire to serve and heal, led me to work myself into the ground. I gave away everything I had until there was nothing left. I burned out physically, emotionally, financially and spiritually. As a result, I had to rebuild my life from the ground up more than once. I was so committed to finding that thread of love in my relationships and healing the traumatised men I partnered up with that I moved states and even continents for them. I left everything behind, even my home country, and ended up on the other side of the world, in Australia.

I had no boundaries, no sense of self. Not even the awareness that the concept of boundaries even existed. How could I? Every part of me had been violated since the moment I was born. In the environment I grew up in, boundaries simply didn't exist.

Then came the moment that completely broke me, the relationship with my daughter's father. His dysfunctional actions, his emotional and psychological abuse, were the final straw that broke my spirit's back. I had lost my identity and the will to live. While I was at my most vulnerable, being pregnant with his child, he dismantled my support network and chipped away at my already low self-esteem. He attacked the very core of my being, my very soul, my mission to heal and to bring love and peace to this world. My optimistic servitude was a thorn in his eyes, and it needed to be destroyed. He succeeded. I found myself in a helpless and hopeless state of deep despair. Then the lights went out, and there was no-one home in my body anymore. I had checked out. Now I was truly alone, not just physically but, to my horror, spiritually. I had lost my connection to source energy and my ability to see the potential in everything. I died. Internally.

And that was the best thing that ever happened to me. As unbearable as that was, he became the catalyst for my ultimate transformation. I died to myself. I died to the identity I was given at birth. All of it vanished. It disappeared. Because somehow in that very dark space, in the depth of my despair, where nothing was left anymore, I found myself. The true me. A light that shone so bright it creates universes.

I came to a powerful realisation that the love my grandmothers shared with me, the unbreakable thread of love that they had passed down through generations, was a love I carried in my own heart all along. The love I had longed for in all of my relationships with others was not something I would ever find in someone else. And I understood that just loving someone isn't enough. I needed to love myself first, unconditionally. This love, pure, unwavering and unconditional, was always there, waiting for me to recognise it, embrace it and allow it to guide me to healing. So, I began loving myself, and with that came the boundaries, which are such an essential part of healing.

When I became a mother, my healing intensified. The birth of my daughter opened me up to even deeper layers of trauma. It was then that I began healing my own inner child, as well as healing the wounds of my ancestors, compiling all the knowledge I had gathered from scientific and ancient materials and applying it to heal my and my ancestors' traumatic experiences. As I did, I experienced profound shifts within myself, truly unlocking the power of unconditional love, for myself and for others. The love I have for my daughter is a continuation of the love that had been passed down to me through my grandmothers. It was here that the thread of love began to shine and grow. It grew deep, strong roots, grounding me in the present and spreading its love throughout my entire family lineage past, present, and future. The thread even wove its way around my mother and all those who had also gotten lost along the way.

I knew then that I had broken the cycle and healed the wounds of trauma, and by doing so, I have passed on this glowing thread of love to my daughter. She now carries it with the same strength and importance I did at her age, but this time, without the pain. Together, we are carrying on the legacy of love, healing and hope.

These days, I live with an incredible sense of peace. The layers of trauma that once clouded my heart have lifted, and within me exists a sanctuary of calm. This stillness isn't the absence of emotion, but rather the presence of inner harmony, a space where I can simply be: whole, balanced, and at peace with who I was, where I came from and who I truly am.

This sense of peace, however, didn't come easily or quickly, but was the result of deep, intentional healing and years of research. A process that went beyond the limits of traditional medicine and psychology and the temporary fixes of medication. Through all of my studies and personal experiences, I discovered early on that psychology alone cannot undo the effects of trauma that are stored in the body. And medication can mask the symptoms for a little while, but it doesn't resolve the underlying causes. True healing begins within the very fabric of your being, the cellular memory of your body.

The problem we are facing today is that medical professionals are well-equipped for treating the biomedical aspects of care, but there is a significant gap in addressing the psychological, cultural and spiritual dimensions of ill-ness and especially trauma. This gap leaves many people feeling lost, disconnected and unsupported, particularly when it comes to the devastating effects of trauma and abuse on the body and the psyche. And medical professionals, as trained as they are, are often not emotionally equipped to connect with their patients in a meaningful way. They are not trained to help patients through the challenges of life that go beyond the physical body, such as emotional pain, spiritual yearning and the need for deeper meaning. Through personal experience and supporting my own clients over the years, I have found that this lack of support leads to a deep sense of unrest within the psyche, leaving many feeling hopeless, helpless and even depressed.

I came to realise the profound importance of emotional intelligence, not just in myself, but in the way we connected with each other. True healing comes when we learn to see beyond the surface, to truly see people, to acknowledge their pain and honour who they are. When we can connect emotionally and spiritually, we offer more than sympathy; we offer understanding and empathy. It's in this deep connection that the pain begins to shift.

For so long, I had been taught that emotions were dangerous, something to be suppressed in order to survive. But through my own experiences, I came to understand that emotions are not something to fear. In fact, they are incredibly powerful and healing when expressed. Emotional intelligence, the ability to understand, manage, and express emotions in a healthy way is the very key to lasting healing. It is what creates peace within ourselves and fosters peaceful living in the world around us. When we embrace and express our emotions authentically, we break the chains of fear and disconnection, allowing ourselves and others to heal and grow.

And thanks to the emerging science of epigenetics and the latest neuroscience, we are beginning to understand the important role emotional intelligence plays in our healing. We also learn that we have the ability to heal at the cellular level by uncovering the root causes of ill-ness without invasive treatments. Because, within the very building block of your DNA lies the key to unlock great health, the meaning of life and your true purpose.

In my work, I bridge that gap between the biomedical and the psychological, cultural and spiritual dimensions of physical and mental ill-ness. Over the years of working in my practice and helping my clients overcome their personal challenges, I have developed a simple somatic healing system called 'The SOAR Process', which works with the body's innate wisdom to uncover and release the trauma stored within. This process doesn't treat any symptoms; instead, it offers understanding as to why an ill-ness occurred in the first place and works to heal it from the root. It also helps my clients tap into the wisdom of their higher selves and align with the universe's love and guidance.

The SOAR Process has transformed my life and helped thousands of clients heal, grow, and thrive in ways they never imagined. Through this process, I have come to understand that my work begins where traditional psychology ends. Psychology, on its own, is simply not enough to heal the deeper, cellular layers of trauma that many of us carry. Medication, while helpful in some cases, is only a temporary fix. But to truly heal, to live a trigger-free life, we must address the root causes of any ill-ness, at the cellular level.

It's been a process of breaking a lot of cycles, of healing the past and of stepping into my true power. Today, I am here to guide others on their own healing journey. I've worked with so many beautiful people, helping them release their trauma and step into lives filled with love, peace and authenticity. It fills my heart with immense joy to witness their transformation, to see them move from fear into love, from pain into freedom and from chaos into peace.

And if I may, leave you, dear reader, with one piece of wisdom, it would be to look for the thread of love in your life. There is a thread of love somewhere. Please look for it, especially when things feel hard, when the weight of life becomes overwhelming. Focus on the one person who embodies that thread of love. It doesn't matter how distant they may seem or how unrelated they might be; there is always someone, somewhere, who carries that glowing love in their heart. If you can't think of anyone right now, I invite you to close your eyes and turn your attention inward. Look at your chest from within, and I promise you, you will find a shining light in the very centre of your being. This light illuminates your presence. It is the essence of love that resides within you.

THE BACKYARD PEACE PROJECT: VOL 1

You are that essence. You are that love. You are never separated from it, and it will never abandon you. Whenever you feel lost or disconnected, remember that love is always within you, guiding you, supporting you and lighting your way.

You are loved.

ABOUT VIRGINIE

Virginie Esprit is a leading-edge healing facilitator, bridging ancient wisdom and modern science to support deep, lasting transformation. As the creator of the SOAR Process, Virginie guides highly sensitive people, empaths and neurodiverse individuals through powerful journeys of trauma healing, emotional freedom and spiritual awakening.

Her multidimensional approach blends neuroscience, epigenetics, quantum energy medicine and spiritual mentorship to release intergenerational trauma, regulate the nervous system, and unlock a deeper connection to one's soul mission.

With over thirty years of experience in leadership, education and holistic wellness across the corporate and private sectors, Virginie has trained more than 2,600 healing professionals worldwide. Many have gone on to become powerful change makers in their own right – running wellness practices, publishing books and opening healing centres around the globe.

Originally from Germany and now based on the east coast of Australia, Virginie's mission is clear: To help sensitive souls rise from fear into love, from disconnection into remembrance, and from pain into purpose.

Healing happens daily – when we return to who we really are.

virginieesprit.com

DR WENDEL NOORDZIJ
PAWS FOR PEACE

I remember one night, laying on my bed, staring blankly at the ceiling as tears quietly soaked my pillow. My body had given up on trying to carry the weight of it all. The room was dim, the silence thick and everything in me had gone quiet. But they didn't flinch. One curled up beside my ribs, the other pressed herself gently behind my knees – a little heartbeat against my skin. No words. No demands. Just fur and breath.

I don't remember how long we lay there. But I do remember their warmth, and the way their eyes watched me, not with pity, not with panic but with a kind of calm expectancy. As if they knew I would get up. As if they were already holding the space for that return.

In that moment, I chose to stay. Not for me. For them. Because they believed I would.

It was one of the most challenging times of my life. My red-flag-filled marriage had ended in a haphazard, painfully inelegant way. And as usual, I hadn't planned ahead. I hadn't anticipated the treats, the fierceness, the abruptness, and I was left overnight without an income, without savings, without a home … and with a 100k debt.

The situation was pretty bleak. I was in the middle of adrenal burnout, a neurodivergent personality crisis and a total collapse of reality. My nervous system was scrambled, my identity scattered and my trust in myself, in justice, and in life, obliterated.

It was too much for my mind to hold.

Everything stopped. I couldn't do this anymore. Even if I wanted to.

A chilling calm came over me, the kind of peace that sits in the centre of a tornado. It became my safe haven at times, and paradoxically, my prison at others. A debilitating daze … yet sometimes, strangely, a quiet and peaceful suspension in space. I could go hours without speaking. Days without real thought. It was as if my system had powered down, preserving just enough energy to keep breathing.

Justice had failed me. Unfairness bled into everything. It felt like the fight of my life, but I didn't even know who or what I was fighting anymore. The system? Him? Myself? Life? The Universe?

What was true? Is there even such a thing as 'the only truth'?

I absolutely knew myself to be a perfectly flawed human being, yet utterly compassionate, self-aware and accountable. So, how on earth did I end up here? I'd studied personal development. I'd worked with spiritual tools. I'd helped others through their darkest hours.

I knew about the universal laws. I understood mirroring, projection, and frequency. But none of it seemed to apply. None of it held.

And so, I stopped trying to give meaning to things. I had to give over and trust, not in the outcome, not in fairness, not in life as I had known it, but in the presence of my breath. Right here. In the moment. In the glimmers of a blissful presence that I could not explain but could feel.

I remember sitting behind a window, staring out into the space on the other side of the glass. Everything outside was alive: the grass was growing, the branches were gently swaying and the leaves were dancing freely in the wind. Flowers had opened in their unique shapes and brightest colours, birds flew in and out at will, flowing through the air, playing in the thermodynamics as if nothing had happened. As if nothing was wrong.

And I just sat there. Deadly still. My body unmoving. My face expressionless.

There was nothing left inside me. Empty of good. Empty of bad. Just … blank. Perfect nothingness remained.

I sat at the edge of existence, not dramatic, not defiant, just ... done. Balancing on the fine thread between a peaceful silence and the silent scream of total despair. Like a spiderweb between two worlds, waiting to dissolve.

And yet, something in me, the tiniest flicker, was still breathing.

I knew I wasn't afraid of death. It felt simpler. Easier. Clean, even. But the universe had so exquisitely orchestrated my need to stay, because I had a rhythm to keep.

Breathe in. Breathe out. For them.

I couldn't leave them. When nobody else did, my girls needed me.

And so I stayed. Not from courage. Not from hope. But because of something simpler than both – responsibility wrapped in love.

I woke because they needed me. I breathed because they did. And in their presence, I remembered mine. I remember their glistening, dark, round eyes looking up at me, not with confusion or fear, but with absolute trust. Blissfully unaware of our looming eviction. Oblivious to the bank balance, the debt, the bills or the sound of my breath catching in the early hours of the morning.

They sat beside me as if everything was fine. And it was. Everything was just fine. I would sit down on the floor with them, and they would press themselves into me. They let me stroke their soft, curly fur for hours, patient, still, unwavering. I could feel their tiny hearts beating beneath their little ribs, pulsing with a quiet rhythm that reminded me I was still here, too.

Sometimes I'd fall asleep on the sofa with one tucked behind my knees, the other curled under my arm. Their soft breath on my skin. Their little inside barks as they dreamt. That was it, the whole reason I was still here.

They had complete trust in me to look after them, no matter what. And somehow, that gave me enough strength to try.

I didn't have answers. I didn't have a plan. But I had them. And in a world that felt like it had slipped out from under me, they were my solid ground.

They didn't need me to be fixed.

They just needed me to stay.

Without a penny to my name and facing imminent homelessness, I used up every forgotten tin, every dusty out-of-date packet of dried food from the back of the cupboards. They now sat, quite peacefully, empty. I opened the doors out of habit, more than hope, as if something might appear.

Yes, I could have asked friends to feed me – and I knew they would have. But instead, I surrendered quietly to a few days without food before borrowing money to buy some more. It wasn't a protest. It wasn't punishment. It just … was. And rather than feeling ravenous, fearful or desperate, it felt like I was reclaiming something. Calmly. Silently. Peacefully.

The eye of the storm.

Without the distraction of food, something new arrived. A clarity. Peace spread through every cell of my being like warm light. I could feel my body again, not as a burden, but as a space. A temple. A living breath.

Presence was never loud. It didn't announce itself with thunder or clarity. It whispered. Through my breath. Through the stillness. Through the steady, quiet rhythm of simply being.

I had no idea this strength was inside of me.

The emptiness reminded me of another time, that hollow ache after my mum died suddenly, when I was just twelve. That kind of grief leaves a silence so vast, it rearranges everything. And yet … I coped.

One breath at a time. No explanations. No rescue. Just breath.

So why would this be different?

Back then, I had nothing left. And still, I survived. Not because I knew how. But because something in me understood: life continues. Even in pain. Even in the void. Even when you don't want it to. This was the same. There was no plan. There was no rescue.

But there was presence.

A clarity came over me, crystal clear. I didn't need anything in that moment. No plan. No promise. No one to save me. I just needed to stay present. To breathe.

To not leave my self.

In that presence, my power returned. Not the forceful kind, not the 'get up and conquer' kind.

A quieter power.

The power of acceptance. Of surrender. Of noticing true beauty. Of releasing control.

Peace arrived not as a reward, but as a consequence of letting go.

A gentle snore behind me. A warm body curled against my legs. A squeaky toy squirrel dropped at my feet with an expectant tail wag. Each day, a little more life. Each breath, a little more space.

I chose breath. Every day. And each step beside my fur babies softened me.

Peace didn't come as a feeling. It came as a decision. Over and over.

My mantra: 'Be present. Be present. Be present.'

And presence began to shape the rhythm of our days. We woke early. Two bowls clinked on the kitchen floor. A quick sniff at the window. A little dance of paws when I reached for their leads. We walked slowly. Stopping for scents, sun patches, and the curiosity of crows.

Some days, I'd sit on the ground in a random field and cry quietly into the grass while they explored nearby, returning every few minutes to nuzzle my arm as if to say, 'Still here. Still with you.'

Inside this spaciousness, dancing became a lifeline too. When I danced, the world disappeared. There were no debts, no evictions, no taunts, no past regrets or looming fears.

Only movement. Only rhythm.

I felt suspended in a peace so graceful, so full of life, that I could live an entire lifetime in a single track of music. Completely present. Cutting through all layers of existence. Tasting the essence of each moment.

It was the same with my dogs. Their eyes would meet mine, and time would stop. No words. Just presence. Just being.

And in those moments, the unbearable became liveable. I began waking up and counting my blessings. Every day. Not in a performative way. Not to manifest anything.

Just because I wanted to remember that we were still here.

We had each other. The steady rhythm of two meals a day. Walks. Cuddles. Play. Sleeping with their warm bodies curled against either side of my legs. That was peace.

And it was enough.

I was no longer merely surviving. I was beginning to live. Not in grand gestures, but in the way I responded to life. In the way I paused before reacting. In the way I breathed through uncertainty. In the way I walked slowed, noticed more, and no longer apologised for needing space.

I started listening from the inside – gently, intuitively – and even guiding others again. Not with answers, but with presence. My inner strength had returned. This became the seed of my work. I now guide others not by giving them steps to follow, but by helping them listen for their own rhythm. To pause. To stay. To find peace, not as a concept, but as a state of being.

Not from fixing. Not from proving. But from authenticity. From peace.

The paws that once tethered me gave way to spreading my wings. I stayed for them. But I kept going for all three of us.

There was a day I noticed it – the shift. It wasn't a single event. It was in the way my breath had become deeper. The way my shoulders no longer lived by my ears. The way life, even in its rawness, began to feel like home. Like opening your eyes on a sunlit morning. That moment when the air is soft and something inside you says: 'Today, you can be you.'

I remember dancing to a song I hadn't heard in years – barefoot, laughing, not because everything was perfect, but because I was here. And here was finally enough. I was finally enough.

We sit together now in silence. Breath to breath.

Peace isn't far. It's in every breath. It always is. It always was.

As I sit here now, two warm bodies pressed against my legs, I feel the ripple of that peace – a quiet, gentle expansion from my chest outward. This is why I now share my story as a global ambassador and advisory board member for the Backyard Peace Project – because I know that the smallest moments of inner stillness, like paws against my legs or a quiet breath, have the power to ripple outward and touch lives we may never meet.

Like a pebble dropped into still water. Each breath, each pause I chose, became part of a ripple. Not just for me, but for every man and woman I now hold space for – because peace doesn't stay still. It travels.

Like light filling the corners of a room. Like breath – invisible, but always present.

What began as survival became something holy. Sacred, even. Not dramatic. Not loud. Just a life. A quiet, chosen life.

Peace, for me, wasn't a breakthrough. It was a soft decision made over and over – to stay, to breathe, to listen for life in the silence.

My dogs never needed me to rise or shine or be anything other than here. And maybe that's what saved me. In their presence, I learnt how to return to mine. And slowly, the unbearable became liveable. The liveable became meaningful. And the meaningful … became peace.

Today, this is the ground from which I support others. Not to fix them, but to sit beside them, hold space and let peace do what it always does – expand.

If you are where I was – raw, tired or on the edge of turning away

DR WENDEL NOORDZIJ

– know this: Peace doesn't ask you to be ready. It just asks you to stay. Because in your staying, something truly special begins. And perhaps – like me – you'll one day look back and realise that a conscious moment of breath can be the start of the you that you were always meant to be.

ABOUT DR WENDEL

My purpose is to help people bring a new way of living, loving and leading – free from the constraints of conditioning.

I believe everyone has it within them to free themselves and consciously create new desired outcomes, and I'm thrilled to be an advisory board member to the Backyard Peace Project.

I'm Dr Wendel, author of the *Paradigm Inversion Method*.

My work and research are built on a simple truth: the most powerful changes don't start with doing more – they start with changing the energy you bring to everything you do, as discovered by some of history's greatest minds around quantum physics, quantum energy and the understanding of frequencies.

Over the years, I've worked with leaders, founders and high achievers who reached a point where success alone wasn't enough. They wanted deeper clarity, stronger relationships, quicker change, better health and the freedom to choose their next chapter from a place of certainty.

Now I'm giving back as much as I can to help as many people as possible so they can lead with more impact, live with more ease and create results that last.

It is such a privilege to be part of the Backyard Peace Project and the

DR WENDEL NOORDZIJ

wonderful work it undertakes around the world.

thedoctorwendel.com
email: connect@TheDoctorWendel.com

JOIN THE MOVEMENT FOR PEACE, CONNECTION, AND CHANGE

Reading these stories is just the beginning. The Backyard Peace Project is a global movement born in South Australia with a bold mission: to turn struggle into strength and create ripple effects of peace that start in our own backyards and spread across the world.

Inside our community, you'll find masterclasses, healing sessions, courageous conversations and a powerful network of people just like you: leaders, parents, creators and dreamers who are ready to choose a different way forward. Together, we are breaking cycles, dissolving isolation and building a future where connection, compassion and courage are the norm.

If these pages spoke to you, don't let the feeling fade. Take your next step toward peace today.

Become a Backyard Peace Project member – connect, grow and help create the world you want to live in.

Scan the QR code to connect with us – The movement is waiting, and so is the version of you who is ready to rise.

Quisk is a creative design studio offering branding, graphic design, web design, SEO, coaching and mentoring and illustration services. Established in 2006, the business began as a home-based business and has steadily grown through a focus on strong relationships and high-quality design work. From the start, the goal has been to help businesses stand out and grow through meaningful, well-crafted branding and digital solutions.

A strong team of talented professionals, Quisk continues to evolve while staying true to its core principles. The studio's values centre on helping and supporting businesses, partnering closely with clients to understand their goals, build their brands and create design outcomes that deliver long-term impact. Whether developing a new brand identity, refreshing an existing one, or creating engaging digital experiences, Quisk works with care and intention to achieve results that make a difference.

Their culture is vibrant and collaborative, with a passion for creativity and an appreciation for clever, timeless design. The studio environment reflects this personality, with colourful, lively details and a warm, welcoming atmosphere that encourages ideas and innovation.

Quisk takes pride in designing with integrity and character, providing not just creative work but genuine support and guidance. By blending strategy, design and a deep commitment to client success, they aim to make a positive and lasting contribution to the businesses they serve. The Quisk approach is about more than design, it's about building partnerships and helping businesses flourish.

quisk.com.au

www.ingramcontent.com/pod-product-compliance
Lightning Source LLC
Chambersburg PA
CBHW022046290426
44109CB00014B/998